FOUNDATION ROLE PLAYS

FOR AUTISM

of related interest

Acting Antics
A Theatrical Approach to Teaching Social Understanding to Kids and Teens with Asperger Syndrome
Cindy B. Schneider
Foreword by Tony Attwood
ISBN 978 1 84310 845 0

Group Interventions for Children with Autism Spectrum Disorders
A Focus on Social Competency and Social Skills
Albert J. Cotugno
ISBN 978 1 84310 910 5

Social Skills for Teenagers and Adults with Asperger Syndrome
A Practical Guide to Day-to-Day Life
Nancy J. Patrick
ISBN 978 1 84310 876 4

Hints and Tips for Helping Children with Autism Spectrum Disorders
Useful Strategies for Home, School, and the Community
Dion E. Betts and Nancy J. Patrick
ISBN 978 1 84310 896 2

FOUNDATION ROLE PLAYS
FOR AUTISM

Role Plays for Working with Individuals with Autism Spectrum
Disorders, Parents, Peers, Teachers and Other Professionals

Andrew Nelson

Jessica Kingsley Publishers
London and Philadelphia

First published in 2010
by Jessica Kingsley Publishers
116 Pentonville Road
London N1 9JB, UK
and
400 Market Street, Suite 400
Philadelphia, PA 19106, USA

www.jkp.com

Library of Congress Cataloging in Publication Data
Nelson, Andrew, 1978-
  Foundation role plays for autism : role plays for working with individuals with autism spectrum disorders, parents, peers, teachers, and other professionals / Andrew Nelson.
      p. ; cm.
  Includes bibliographical references.
  ISBN 978-1-84905-063-0 (alk. paper)
  1. Autism spectrum disorders--Treatment. 2. Autistic children. 3. Role playing in children--Therapeutic use. I. Title.
  [DNLM: 1. Autistic Disorder--therapy. 2. Adolescent. 3. Child. 4. Role Playing. WS 350.6 N424f 2010]
  RJ506.A9N435 2010
  618.92'891523--dc22

                                  2009039782

British Library Cataloguing in Publication Data
A CIP catalogue record for this book is available from the British Library

ISBN 978 1 84905 063 0

Printed and bound in the United States by
Thomson-Shore, 7300 Joy Road, Dexter, MI 48130

Dedicated to Nathaniel Gray, Beth Isakson, and the great teachers at Behavioral Dimensions, Inc.

ACKNOWLEDGMENTS

I wish to briefly thank some of the people who helped inspire, nurture, and refine many of the concepts in this book. First, thank you to Dr. Barbara Becker-Cottrill, Charlotte Hays, and my many friends at the West Virginia Autism Training Center for creating an environment of exploration, and for teaching me the PBS person-centered philosophy. Profound thanks to my dear friend and mentor Dr. Parasuram Ramamoorthi for his guidance and support. And most importantly, thank you to the families and teachers in Minnesota, West Virginia, and Madurai for your willingness to let go of inhibitions and role play in order to better support and understand our friends on the autism spectrum.

CONTENTS

* denotes role-playing CD tracks

FOREWORD

When thinking back to my own childhood, I have a vivid picture of the many role-playing experiences I shared with my siblings, classmates and friends at different periods. As is typical of early childhood, my first memories are of role-playing familiar events closely tied to the reality of day-to-day life. Clomping around in wooden shoes given to us by our grandparents, I remember pretending to be a Dutch family with my big sister and brother and two baby sisters. Although I at first coveted the role of mommy—which was naturally preordained for my older sister—I was easily swayed to role-play the eldest of the three daughters—a rare opportunity for the eternal middle-child. While we busied ourselves with typical family scenarios—shopping, cooking, bedtime rituals and the like—I gained insight into familial order as the make-believe mature, older sister.

Inspired by books and films in later years, role playing transported us to new and different worlds, real and imagined. We traveled back-and-forth through time, trekking across continents, exploring the deepest crevices of the earth and the most outer limits of space. The narratives we co-created in fantasy allowed us try on many new hats, rich with archetypes of our impending realities. A favorite theme we repeated often was motivated by the tales of Peter Pan and Oliver Twist:

> I remember as a little girl playing runaway orphans with my two younger sisters and a neighborhood friend … We gathered together all our dolls and stuffed animals in blankets. My one sister brought along Mr. Peabody, her imaginary friend. Together we set out to explore the "never-never land" of all the backyards in the neighborhood. Every step of the way we encountered a new adventure—imagining near escapes from evil foes, seeking refuge in forts of leaves and snow (*Play and Imagination in Children with Autism* - Wolfberg 2009, p. 27).

While growing older, role playing took on new meaning for sorting out the complexities of relationships and our own social, cultural and moral identities within a dynamic and ever-changing society. An especially profound recollection was the classic sociological role-playing exercise of being stranded on a deserted island. Initiated by my 7th grade social studies teacher, the class was assigned the task of formulating a plan for survival given some basic, albeit insufficient, food, water and supplies to sustain everyone. The teacher merely sat back and observed. It was an emotionally-charged event that revealed divergent facets of human nature in especially raw and visceral ways. I was quickly reminded of the classic story *Lord of the Flies* as the attempt to create order erupted quickly into chaos and conflict. In my self-assigned role as benevolent community member, it was invigorating to speak out against those who took dictatorial roles motivated by self-interest. Although frustrated by my fruitless attempts to sway the tribes to take a different path, the experience was formative in helping to shape my direction in life, both personally and professionally.

Ultimately, it is the accumulation of such role-playing experiences that enables us to figure out life's many lessons in preparation for adulthood. Role playing offers fertile ground for trying out new roles while building skills needed for acquiring social competence. On a more basic level, we learn how to effectively communicate, socialize, play and form mutual friendships. On a more sophisticated level, we learn how to interpret social cues, appreciate one another's perspectives, regulate emotions, develop empathy, negotiate and compromise to resolve conflicts, address issues of social status, intimacy and trust, and the unspoken rules of the peer culture.

Andrew Nelson's timely book, *Foundation Role Plays for Autism* is aimed at helping individuals on the autism spectrum access the many benefits afforded by role playing. Autism is a complex neurological condition that affects capacities to interact socially with others, communicate basic needs, feelings and ideas, understand and use language effectively, develop play and imagination, and form peer relationships. Through a variety of thoughtful, creative and fun role-play activities, this book offers a portal to overcoming the unique and complex challenges these individuals may face in many aspects of their lives. This sensitive volume reaches out to not only individuals on the autism spectrum, but also their broader social network including families, peers, teachers and other professionals. I look forward to the joy of passing on this important work to the many people in my professional community where role playing is certain to impact generations to come.

Pamela Wolfberg, Ph.D., Associate Professor and Director
Autism Spectrum Program, San Francisco State University and
Autism Institute on Peer Relations and Play www.wolfberg.com

INTRODUCTION

Before I became interested in working with individuals with autism, my training and passion was in drama. Several years were spent playing different roles, assuming new perspectives, and exploring psychology through performance. At the time I had no idea that the work I was doing was laying the foundation for my own development as a student of autism.

A dear friend convinced me to come to work with him at an early intensive behavioral intervention company that used applied behavior analysis to build communication and social skills with children with autism. I was fortunate enough to be hired by this company and was sent through their rigorous staff training sequence before meeting any children.

A major component of their training was role playing. Role play was used creatively to prepare for challenging situations and behaviors, deliver reinforcement, establish behavioral contingencies, shape communication, redirect and prompt, and many other skills that the job required. As I look back at that amazing training, I realize how important the role-playing of job skills was for my self-confidence and overall competency as a teacher. A connection was made between my training as an actor and my new-found passion for teaching children with autism via role play.

Since that time I have been able to use role play to teach other teachers and parents of individuals with autism some of the same skills I acquired during my training. The smiles, laughter, discussions, ideas, epiphanies, and self-confidence I have witnessed others find through role play inspired me to put some of the scenarios down on paper. I hope that you or someone you know can benefit from the strategies offered in this book.

Role play for student, teacher, parent, and peer development has several positive aspects that deserve mentioning. First, role-playing a new skill or scenario can be a lot of *fun*! It is liberating to walk in someone else's shoes or take risks you might not take in the real world. Feeling free to make mistakes and bold choices leads to new ground, and finding new ground usually feels good.

Making bold choices, however, would not be possible without the *safe* environment that role play helps to establish. When mindfully executed, role play allows participants to let their guards down and work in the spirit of trust. This feature of role play is hard to find in daily life.

Mistakes are embraced because role play encourages *repeated practice*. In any given scenario, participants can try skills or ideas over and over again until they feel comfortable with them and are ready to move on. We know that individuals with autism may need multiple opportunities to practice new skills before using them, but don't we all?

Part of the reason role play is able to accomplish these things is because it brings *structure* to otherwise abstract and nebulous concepts. Role-play scenarios put situations or skills into a structured framework to help break concepts into manageable pieces. Structure is incredibly important for individuals on the spectrum. Structure is important for any learner.

Role play is *active*. Many of us learn by getting up on our feet and moving, by working through a problem physically. Some training programs for students with ASD are linear and passive. Role play allows people to interact and share space, to actively pursue answers and change.

Role play is a *cost-effective* strategy. School systems, parents, trainers, and others do not have to spend piles of money to use role play for development. In fact, most of the activities in this book require only a writing surface and a writing utensil. We can implement role-play strategies quickly without having to spend precious resources, other than time and creativity, to do so.

Finally, and most importantly, *role-play activities emphasize strengths.* We have all read or heard about what we as parents, teachers, peers, or individuals on the spectrum cannot do or do not do well. Most of the activities in this book ask "What can we do to ensure a better future?" and "What positive things can we use to build on?" This is a critical point which we cannot forget.

RESEARCH ON THE USE OF ROLE PLAY

Role play is certainly a fun and exciting approach, but does it work and how do we know? First, we must consider the research on the ethical considerations when using role play. Since role play deals with the self and self-development, great care on the part of the facilitator must be given to the psychological and philosophical aspects of the role play (Jones 2008). Role play should always be voluntary, and practitioners must be sensitive to the messages sent when asking someone to join in a role-play scenario (Nicholson 2005). Some have used role play itself to examine ethical issues (Kraus 2008), and using role play to examine the ethics of role play may be an interesting exercise.

Why should we try role play with individuals with autism and those who support them? Research indicates that role-play techniques have the power to transform environments into places where individuality is celebrated and caring relationships between students and teachers are cultivated (Pecaski and McLennan 2008). Role play has been used in conjunction with social skills training to help students with autism develop social skills (Chan and O'Reilly 2008). Research specifically highlighting role play for autism is not robust. However, data indicates that role play would be a good fit for individuals on the spectrum. Participants have been able to tie real-world actions to the role-play scenarios (Schick 2008), connect past events to the present (Irwin 1977), understand the perspectives of others, work on daily living skills ("Table Tactics" 2008), and explore feelings and problems in a safe environment (Bielanska, Cechnicki, and Budzyna-Dawidowski 1991). Role play has also been used as an effective assessment tool to measure such things as psychological symptoms (Carlson, Tahiroglu, and Taylor 2008) and social skills performance (Sitzer, Twamley, Patterson and Jeste 2008).

Role play has been used extensively with caregivers such as parents, teachers, doctors, and psychologists to improve skills. Teachers have been trained to implement strategies using role play and feedback (Roscoe and Fisher 2008), and role-play participants often outperform control groups who have not used role-play techniques (Ahsen 2008). Participants report that role play has helped them empathize with those experiencing mental health issues (Ballon, Silver, and Fidler 2007) and that role play increased feelings of self-confidence and competence (Eckstrom *et al.* 2008). Medical students have been taught the skills needed to deliver upsetting news (Baer *et al.* 2008) as well as skills such as listening to a patient's concerns and maintaining confidentiality (Hardoff and Schonmann 2001) through role play. Role play has also been used for leadership preparation (Meltzer

2002), communication training (Jacobsen *et al.* 2006), and social worker training (Balen and Masson 2008). Parents are no exception as role-play techniques have been used to teach essential parenting skills as well (Berard and Smith 2008). Finally, research indicates that role play is most effective when scenarios and strategies are practiced *at least monthly* (Rowan 2008).

Data for using role play to incorporate the skills and perspectives of peers is strong. Role play can be used with peers to stimulate thoughtful discussions on a variety of topics (Harding *et al.* 1996; Day 1998), and it gives participants an opportunity to voice and dramatize their needs and concerns (Jackson 2003). Role play has been shown to increase academic skills (Borgia, Owles, and Marcell 2008) and critical social support skills such as protection from peer bullying (Halleck 2008). Positive role-play data exists (Joronen, Rankin, and Astedt-Kurki 2008) but the field has plenty of room for more evidence.

WHEN TO ROLE-PLAY, WHEN TO TRY SOMETHING ELSE

Sometimes role-playing strategies may not be the best option for your student, child, teacher, parent, or peer. Role playing requires voluntary participation which may be difficult to achieve with some participants. Some may need more foundation forming skills in place, such as basic communication and emotional expression, before being able to meet the demands of many of the role-play activities. Periodically you will have to give reluctant participants additional encouragement to get them into a role play at first. Some tough love and strong encouragement is okay for those participants. However, do not force role-players to do something they are unwilling or unable to do. Ask for help from others if you are unsure, and seek alternate activities for participants who may not be ready for role play.

GENERALIZATION OF ROLE-PLAY STRATEGIES

Because we are using role-playing techniques that *simulate* real-life scenarios, careful attention must be paid to make sure we help participants "generalize," or apply, what they learn in role play to their daily lives.

Stokes and Baer (1977) discussed generalization as it related to autism. A handful of generalization techniques have been pulled from this work to give facilitators general tools to use to promote generalization. It is hoped that these basic tips will help increase the likelihood that participants will apply skills from role-play scenarios in real life.

Role play generalization strategy 1

Once we see participants successfully using new skills in role-playing scenarios, we can systematically help that participant to generalize skills to the most natural environment or desired social situation. Example: If a participant struggles with large-group social situations, systematically increase social partners in role-play scenarios or activities until the participant successfully uses his or her new skills in the target group size. Then systematically fade the structure of the role-play activity to more natural structures or situations while maintaining the target group size.

Role play generalization strategy 2

Peers, parents, and teachers can be invited to take part in role-play activities with the participant. Skills being addressed in the activities can be watched for by the peers, parents, or teachers in the natural environment, and spontaneous attempts to use the skills can be reinforced.

Role play generalization strategy 3

We can use role-play activities to train a variety of responses such as social greetings, refusals, interaction repairs, and jokes. Role-play activities can be practiced in and for a variety of settings, either literal or implied. A variety of social partners (peers, teachers, parents, strangers) can be involved in activities so the participant has opportunities to practice skills with multiple people. It may be necessary to start with a "core" of skills that can be used in multiple situations. Example: Start by using role-play activities to teach a handful of ways to greet others, and then expand the list of others the participant is greeting, then begin teaching multiple ways to repair social interactions.

Role play generalization strategy 4

Loose, less structured role plays can be built around "general" topics or skills, allowing the participant to practice multiple scenarios, responses, and strategies in a variety of improvised contexts. Discussion of positive skill use after each improvisation session can help reinforce the occurrence of those skills in future improvisations or real-world scenarios.

Role play generalization strategy 5

Materials from the real-life setting can be brought in as props or set pieces during role-play activities. Example: If problems are occurring in the lunchroom, identical materials (trays, beverages, food, etc.) can be used as props in activities. Peers from the actual lunchroom setting could also be incorporated to role-play the issues that are occurring in the lunchroom. The idea is for the role-play training to mirror the actual stimuli well enough to prepare the participant for situations as they occur in the generalization environment.

Role play generalization strategy 6

Ask the participant to self-record either the successful use of a new skill or the need for more practice, and bring ideas to the group or report events to the teacher or facilitator. Then use role-play activities to practice the skill. After practicing in the role-play setting, have the participant try again in the generalization environment, using self-record or report strategies to monitor success.

Role play generalization strategy 7

Specifically ask questions after role-play activities about how the skills could be used at school, at home, and in the community. Give specific instructions to the participants to try their new skills in the community, at school, or at home. Let them know that you will be asking parents, teachers, and peers to watch for specific skill use and set up a reinforcement system for the participants' generalization to help motivate them.

EXAMPLES FOR SETTING UP A ROLE PLAY

It is hoped that breaking down the process of creating a role-play scenario into small steps will help you understand how the role plays in this book were designed, as well as how to create your own role-play scenarios. The example of Amy and her scenario will be referenced throughout this section to show a real-world case in which the following information was applied. Each role play has been based on the simple sequence: Who–What–Where–How–When. This sequence can be used to structure any role play you may need to design and implement.

Who

The first step is asking yourself who you are aiming to support with a role play. For example, this could be a parent, student, peer, bus driver, coach, a group of people. *Amy was a 10-year-old girl with Asperger Syndrome who attended a public school I was working in.*

What

Next, you must ask yourself what you want the role-play participants to learn or identify through the role play. This could be a new social skill, a teaching or parenting strategy, or a play skill. *Amy was a very friendly girl who was witty and well-liked by her peers. She believed that "no one liked her" despite many peers approaching her and initiating social interactions or play. I wanted to teach her how to recognize friendly social signals from peers/friends.*

Where

Next, observe your target role-playing individual or group as much as possible and ask where the situation most often occurs. Then build your role play to resemble that environment as much as possible. The role-playing environment could resemble, for example, a store, bus, bedroom, sporting event. *Amy was being approached by friendly peers mostly during lunch and recess, so we set up the role play to resemble those two environments by bringing in lunch trays and utensils and toys from the playground.*

How

Next, plans must address how the role play will be presented. By this time you will know who you are working with, what skill or situation you are addressing, and what environment you are trying to emulate. So, you will next have to decide how you want to go about your role play. How will you incorporate teaching materials; how will you use pre-discussion to set a context for the role players; how will you add elements systematically to the role play; and how will you use follow-up discussions to synthesize what was learned? *Amy needed help to decode when peers were giving her friendly cues in the lunchroom and on the playground. I began by facilitating a few questions to get a better understanding of Amy's perspective. Then we discussed and demonstrated what a friendly body and face looked like. After practicing and demonstrating the friendly signals, we incorporated some props from each environment (lunchroom, playground) and began the role play. Amy's mother and I played the role of the peers as school was out for the summer and peers were not available. We practiced many situations where peers approached Amy and gave her a variety of social cues. After each situation we quickly asked Amy if the signal was friendly or unfriendly. We ended the role play with a brief summarizing discussion and I gave Amy the homework of finding friendly faces in the community grocery store and taking some notes about how they appeared.*

When

Finally, you as a facilitator need to help decide when this role play will be executed. Will you repeat the role play over many weeks or months? Will you run the scenario in the morning before lunchroom challenges arise? Careful thought should be given to slowly fading out the role play and promoting generalization as much as possible. Set specific times to run the role play and help ensure involvement by setting a schedule that role-play participants can follow. *Amy initially role-played her scenario in the summer. We set a follow-up role play just before school started and met with the teacher to role-play one or two more times at the beginning of the school year, this time incorporating peers from school to make the role play more authentic.*

TIPS FOR USING THIS BOOK

Foundation Role Plays for Autism was designed so that virtually anyone can pick up an activity and facilitate without needing hours of training. I hope that you will feel comfortable trying a wide variety of the activities in this book with a wide variety of participants.

Also, this book was designed to allow the reader to make the role-playing process truly their own. Chapter 5 of this book has blank, photocopy-friendly forms that you can use to design your own role-playing activities. After using a few of the activities in the book you should be able to get a sense for how to set up an activity and then design one to fit the needs of the participants you serve. The range of activities in this book is by no means exhaustive and you will almost certainly need to create new, individualized activities.

You will occasionally find activities repeated for each role-playing group, most often repeated in the sections for teachers/caregivers and parents. This is by design. As we know, with autism a consistent approach is a must. Using similar role-playing activities with teachers and parents should help teams develop a more consistent approach to supporting individuals with autism. Also, repeating and modifying activities across each group gives teams a "vocabulary of activities" they can use together at any time, anywhere.

Role-playing activities can be used to bring teams together in good times and stressful times. Experience has shown that role play can take pressure off teams, allowing them to step back and examine situations with a fresh perspective. So bring as many people together as possible to role-play and have fun!

Chapter 1

ROLE PLAY FOR INDIVIDUALS ON THE AUTISM SPECTRUM

Case Study: Mark's Tough Day Playback

One day a colleague and I received an email from the parent of a young man, Mark, whom we had spent a lot of time with over the years. Mark's mom, teacher, and employer were concerned about an incident that had happened at his work program. The email described a situation where Mark had interacted inappropriately with a peer and had made some of his peers nervous with mild aggressive behavior.

The email shared the challenging event in detail and in sequence. After a day or two had passed we asked Mark if he would be okay if we played out the event and tried to figure out some strategies for interaction in the future. He agreed. We simply took the sequence of events from the email to set a "loose outline" and created opportunities to pause the role play and survey peers for more appropriate solutions to the Tough Day's challenges.

We had Mark watch others do a Tough Day Playback. Two adults role-played as the teachers and supervisors, and Mark's peers played the co-workers. On large sheets of paper we took suggestions from peers for new interaction strategies Mark might try. We then asked each peer to get up and role-play using their suggested strategy. Most of the strategies involved different ways Mark could initiate greetings with others, talk about his interests, and ask other people questions about their day, instead of using aggressive interaction styles. A discussion followed and Mark seemed to leave with a clearer picture of what had happened and what he could try in the future.

After the Tough Day Playback we never received another report from Mark or his supervisors and parents suggesting any of the same challenges. It was a non-threatening, ten-minute, peer-driven role play that helped Mark develop new strategies such as using safe greetings, recognizing when someone is uncomfortable, and asking others about their interests first.

ACTIVITY 1.1: SUPERMARKET SUCCESS

Purpose

To role-play scenarios and skills needed to have a successful trip to a large department store.

Materials needed

CD track 1, CD player, real or play money, real or pretend store items, paper and pencil

People needed

Three or more

Procedure

Begin by asking the group of role-players simple questions about their experiences at supermarkets. Where do you go when you go shopping? What do you like to buy when you go there? What kind of things do you like about stores? What do you dislike? What are the tough things about shopping?

Take notes on a large sheet of white paper or a chalkboard, and write down specific challenges and strengths for each role-player.

Then set up the role-play scenario by telling the players that they will be pretending to go to a supermarket to purchase a few items that they may need in real life. Also inform the players that they will take turns playing the role of shopper, cashier, and floor clerk.

Support each player as they complete the Activity 1.1: Supermarket Success form to help structure the role-play scenario. Facilitate the formation of a list of 1–3 items to purchase, an estimate of how much those items will cost and how much money will be needed to purchase them, greetings and questions for each character, and a list of sensory strategies to handle sensory challenges often present in large store settings.

Then start the CD and begin the role play by choosing who will play which characters. One player should play the shopper, one the cashier, and the remaining players can play floor clerks. Guide the shopper to find the items on his purchase list with the help of floor clerks when needed, purchase the items, and interact with all players successfully. Switch roles and repeat.

Discuss the outcomes, strengths, and areas needing more skill practice.

ACTIVITY 1.1: SUPERMARKET SUCCESS

Shopper

My 1–3 items:

Estimated cost of those items:

How much money I will bring:

Two things I can ask a clerk if i need help:

Two greetings I can use with the cashier:

My sensory challenges and what I can do to prepare for them:

Floor Clerk/Cashier

My job in the store:

Two greetings I can use with shoppers:

Two things I can do in the scenario if I'm not talking to customers:

Two things I can say as the customer leaves the store:

Notes:

ACTIVITY 1.2: FIRST DAY JITTERS

Purpose

To decrease stress related to the first day of school through practice and preparation.

Materials needed

Backpack or bag, sample planner, paper, pencil

People needed

Two or more (depending on needs)

Procedure

Do as much homework as possible about where the new student will be going to school, who the teacher will be, where his classes will be if possible, potential peers, where her locker will be, and so on. Then begin a discussion with the new student about her previous school experiences.

First, facilitate questions about what she likes about school and what she feels her strengths are in school. Have or help her write those strengths on the Activity 1.2: First Day Jitters form. Be sure to incorporate strengths into the role play when possible.

Second, ask questions about the student's concerns going into the first day and have or help her write those concerns on the Activity 1.2: First Day Jitters form.

Third, decide on 1–3 scenarios that you will facilitate with the student and have or help her write those scenarios on the Activity 1.2: First Day Jitters form. For example, "finding my locker" may be a concern. You could role-play carrying the right books to the right class, turning the dial on the locker, or discriminating between sample locker numbers on a wall. Again, the more pre-information you can get from the school, the better (i.e., getting the locker number she will actually have, the combination, etc.)

After role-playing each scenario, have the student write or dictate how the exercise felt and if she feels more prepared to handle each specific concern on the Activity 1.2: First Day Jitters form. If she is still uneasy about a particular topic, dig deeper into the concern or refine the role play and make it more specific.

Finally, close by discussing, documenting on the Activity 1.2: First Day Jitters form, and role-playing strategies the student can use from day one should she experience major difficulties. For example: "Asking to go to the library if I need a quiet place", "Finding a friendly teacher", "Finding a friendly peer", "Asking for help", "Sensory strategies that work for me". The Activity 1.2: First Day Jitters form can be taken to school as a support for the student once she has completed the role-play scenarios and documented strategies.

ACTIVITY 1.2: FIRST DAY JITTERS

Remembering my strengths…

My general concerns are…

Let's practice…

1.

2.

3.

How did that feel? Am I less concerned?

My tips if things don't go as I had planned…

ACTIVITY 1.3: ON THIS ISLAND

Purpose

To build problem-solving skills, cooperation strategies, and flexibility when working with others.

Materials needed

Five simple household or classroom items

People needed

Two or three

Procedure

Select participants for the role play and then have them locate five common items from the immediate environment. Once the items have been selected, begin to set up the framework for the role play.

1. Inform the participants that they will be pretending to be stranded on an island.

2. Explain that the five items they have chosen are the only items they have to get them off of the island.

3. Describe the situation and let them know that they must work together to figure out creative ways to use the items to get off the island.

4. Set Ground Rule 1 that once a participant establishes a use for an item (rubber band = a slingshot, towel = a sail for a boat, etc.), that use must not change and the group must accept it as fact.

5. Set Ground Rule 2 that participants must take turns brainstorming ideas for the uses of each item.

6. Set Ground Rule 3 that if a disagreement occurs, the participants must work together to resolve the issue.

7. Begin the role play and provide support, praise, and feedback when necessary to ensure the participants work together to find a way off the island using the five items.

After finishing, facilitate a conversation about the role play, asking specific questions about what cooperation strategies worked best and what the challenges were. Also, ask how the skills needed in the role play can be used in the participants' daily lives and how they might benefit the participants. Document responses on the Activity 1.3: On This Island form.

ACTIVITY 1.3: ON THIS ISLAND

What cooperation strategies did we use? Which worked well?

What was most challenging?

When can I use these strategies in my real life?

How can these strategies benefit my life?

ACTIVITY 1.4: DEFEND A FRIEND

Purpose

To help participants develop positive strategies when standing up for peers or self, and to give them a chance to implement those strategies.

Materials needed

Writing materials

People needed

Two or more

Procedure

Begin the activity by discussing bullying, teasing, or other negative social interactions the participants may have witnessed or experienced at school or in the community. If appropriate, discuss how those experiences made them feel and what strategies they used to handle those situations. Then, as a group, develop a list of appropriate, non-violent things they can say or do to defend a friend or themselves should they have to. Document suggestions on a large sheet of paper or writing surface placed near the performing area.

Enlist a co-facilitator to help with the next step. Inform the participants that they will be trying out some of their strategies. Model the bullying or teasing with the co-facilitator, and coach the participants to approach the situation and deliver one of the appropriate suggestions listed in the group exercise or one of their own. Then have the participants repeat the process while adding a verbalization or physical move to remove themselves and their peer from the situation. Example: "I don't like the way you're talking to (Sam). Come on (Sam), let's go."

After the role play, have the participants define "bullying." Then begin a discussion about how it felt to stand up for a friend or for themselves when someone was teasing or bullying them. Talk about non-violent solutions to bullying as well. Finally, ask participants to think about who they might talk to should bullying occur.

ACTIVITY 1.4: DEFEND A FRIEND

I define bullying as...

How does it feel to stand up to bullying?

What non-violent strategies can I use?

Who can I talk to about someone bullying me or my friends?

ACTIVITY 1.5: ALL IN THE TIMING

Purpose

To practice appropriately initiating, maintaining, and ending social interactions.

Materials needed

Writing materials for note-taking

People needed

Three or more, with skilled adults/peers to help

Procedure

Begin by informing the participants that they will be working how to start, maintain, and end social interactions. Explain the importance of this skill in life. Facilitate a conversation about a time in their life when they remember a social interaction going well and one going poorly. Then ask each participant to list what they think their social strengths are (good listener, polite, enthusiastic, etc.) on the Activity 1.5: All in the Timing form. Once finished, begin role-playing the various social scenarios for initiating, maintaining, and ending social interactions. Mix in skilled adults or peers to play specific roles when possible.

Initiating with…

1. **Teacher** – when the teacher is: teaching others, alone, talking to another teacher, on the phone.
2. **Peer** – when the peer is: playing a game with others, alone, sitting at the lunch table, talking with another peer.
3. **Parent** – when the parent is: talking to others, alone, on the phone, talking to another parent.

Maintaining with…

1. **Teacher** – staying on topic, accepting a new topic, asking open-ended and closed-ended questions.
2. **Peer** – staying on topic, accepting a new topic, asking open-ended and closed-ended questions.
3. **Parent** – staying on topic, accepting a new topic, asking open-ended and closed-ended questions.

Ending with…

1. **Teacher** – cues that it's ending, closing statements, non-verbal practice.
2. **Peer** – cues that it's ending, closing statements, non-verbal practice.
3. **Parents** – cues that it's ending, closing statements, non-verbal practice.

On the Activity 1.5: All in the Timing form, have the participants document positive cues that others give for social initiation, cues that the interaction is needing a boost, and cues that the interaction is ending. Document verbal and non-verbal strategies for each step in the socialization process as well.

ACTIVITY 1.5: ALL IN THE TIMING

> I think my social strengths are…

> Cues others give for social initiation…
>
> Non-verbal and verbal tips for initiating…

> Cues that the social interaction is changing…
>
> Non-verbal and verbal tips for maintaining…

> Cues that the social interaction is ending…
>
> Non-verbal and verbal tips for ending…

> How do my strengths fit in?

ACTIVITY 1.6: STRANGER SAFETY

Purpose

To practice safe interaction strategies with strangers.

Materials needed

CD tracks 2 and 3 (US), 38 and 39 (British), CD player, writing materials

People needed

One or more

Procedure

Begin a discussion with participants about stranger safety. This conversation can range from basic questions about who is a stranger to more subtle questions about the nature of interacting with strangers. Once you have a sense for what level of understanding the participants have about stranger safety, begin to role-play the following steps.

Go through a list of people ranging from family to community members to strangers, and ask each participant to label them as "friend" or "stranger." Then help participants put each person into a category on the Activity 1.6: Stranger Safety form.

Next, talk about steps the participants can take should a stranger try to get them to come with them. Help each participant develop a safe and simple four-step procedure and document each step on the Activity 1.6: Stranger Safety form.

Then, using either the youth or teen track on the CD, role-play the stranger safety scenario where each participant practices their four-step procedure. The facilitator may need to act as the stranger while the CD plays a simulated stranger's voice. Discuss, refine, and practice the scenario until each participant is fluid with their responses.

Finally, talk with each participant about how some people start off as strangers and become friends over time. Be sure to help participants understand that not all strangers are dangerous, and work together to develop safe interaction strategies to use with strangers. Document these safe stranger interaction strategies on the Activity 1.6: Stranger Safety form. End by role-playing how to use those safe-stranger strategies. Discuss, refine, and practice until the participants are comfortable with their new skills.

ACTIVITY 1.6: STRANGER SAFETY

Friend	Stranger

If a stranger tries to get me to meet or go with them I can…

1.

2.

3.

4.

I can safely interact with strangers by…

ACTIVITY 1.7: CAN I TAKE A MESSAGE?

Purpose

To practice phone answering and message taking skills.

Materials needed

CD tracks 4–6 (US), 40–42 (British), CD player, phone, writing materials

People needed

One or more

Procedure

Begin a conversation with participants about the importance of good phone skills and taking a message. Ask what critical information a phone message has and explain that the role play will help them develop strategies for taking a message.

Step 1 – Greeting

Have participants generate a list of phone greetings they feel comfortable using and have them write these greetings on the Activity 1.7: Can I Take a Message? form. Discuss the importance of a solid greeting and what that communicates to a social partner.

Step 2 – Determining if a message is needed

Talk with participants about what to do if the caller asks for someone who is not home at that time. Help each participant develop a few appropriate responses to use if family members or members of the household are not home. Document these responses on the Activity 1.7: Can I Take a Message? form.

Step 3 – Writing information and ending the call

Encourage participants to practice asking for and writing down the name, number, and other information of the caller. Then help participants develop a list of phrases they can use to end a phone conversation appropriately. Finish preparation by asking participants where they can place phone messages so others can easily find them. Document these phrases and ideas on the Activity 1.7: Can I Take a Message? form.

Step 3 – Role play

Using either the CD call samples or a phone script of your own, practice by having the participants use one of their greetings, determining if a message is needed, receiving and writing the name–number–information of the caller, and placing the message in a place where the family member can find it.

ACTIVITY 1.7: CAN I TAKE A MESSAGE?

When I answer the phone I can say...

If the person the caller is looking for is not home, I can say...

Then I can ask questions and write information...

"May I ask who is calling?"

"What number can they reach you at?"

Other important information

I can end the call by saying...

Where I will put the message so others will see it...

ACTIVITY 1.8: HOME ALONE

Purpose

To role-play various scenarios or skills to increase independence and safety when home alone.

Materials needed

Writing materials

People needed

One or more, parents or caregivers of participants

Procedure

Begin a general conversation with all participants about the independence it takes to stay home alone. Ask questions about current levels of independence regarding staying home alone and how it feels to gain independence and responsibility.

Next, ask participants with autism to think about what makes them anxious, scared, or nervous about staying home alone. You can guide them to think about emergency issues or other safety issues. Have participants document as many concerns as possible on the Activity 1.8: Home Alone form.

Then work with participants to help them complete the statement "I would feel better if…" and find at least 2–4 things that they could practice in role play to help reduce anxieties about being home alone. Document these strategies on the Activity 1.8: Home Alone form.

Now, work with parents and caregivers of the participants to think about what makes *them* anxious or scared about allowing their son or daughter to stay home alone. Reassure parents that it is ultimately their decision when the right time is to take these steps. Have parents document as many concerns as possible on the Activity 1.8: Home Alone form.

Also, allow parents to consider and respond to the statement "I would feel better if…" and find at least 2–4 things they would like to see their son or daughter practice in role play to help reduce anxieties about being home alone. Document these strategies on the Activity 1.8: Home Alone form.

Finally, begin role-play scenarios focusing on the 2–4 items that each participant/parent generated, and start to practice new skills and safety measures in role play. Role-playing in the participant's home is ideal, though not completely necessary. Respond to what worked, change what did not work, and continue to practice new skills in role play to help families work toward greater independence.

ACTIVITY 1.8: HOME ALONE

If I think about being home alone I worry about…

I would feel better if…

1.

2.

3.

4.

If I think about my son or daughter being home alone I worry about…

I would feel better if…

1.

2.

3.

4.

ACTIVITY 1.9: CAFETERIA CUSTOMS

Purpose

To practice social skills related to eating in the cafeteria, and to address any support needs participants may have in the cafeteria.

Materials needed

CD track 7, CD player, cafeteria props, chairs, tables, writing materials

People needed

Between two and ten

Procedure

Start the activity by talking generally about the cafeteria: what is done there, what time of the day we go there, for example. Get participants to talk generally about their feelings regarding lunchtime, their likes and dislikes, and so on.

Next, talk with participants about the school rules that are in place for the cafeteria and document them on the Activity 1.9: Cafeteria Customs form. Discuss why those rules are important and why they are in place.

Then ask participants to think about their lunch experiences and list who they usually sit with, what their peer group likes to talk about, and what they personally like to talk about. Record these on the Activity 1.9: Cafeteria Customs form.

Follow with a discussion about unwritten social rules that people usually follow during mealtimes and while eating lunch in the cafeteria. Have participants think about good ideas, behaviors, and social skills to practice in the cafeteria, as opposed to ideas and behaviors that may not be good to practice at lunch. Document ideas on the Activity 1.9: Cafeteria Customs form.

Ask participants to think of 1–3 things that they would like help with regarding cafeteria issues and document these on the Activity 1.9: Cafeteria Customs form.

Finally, using the information from the form and the CD, begin a role play where participants practice exploring school rules, conversation skills, good ideas versus bad ideas, and any of the 1–3 issues they identified as wanting help with. Give participants opportunities to practice new skills, ask questions, try new ideas, and rehearse difficult situations to better prepare for real-world cafeteria situations.

ACTIVITY 1.9: CAFETERIA CUSTOMS

The school rules in my cafeteria are…

I usually sit at a table with…

The people at my table like to talk about…

I like to talk about…

It is a good idea to…

It is not a good idea to…

I would like help with…

1.

2.

3.

ACTIVITY 1.10: TOUGH DAY PLAYBACK

Purpose

To talk through an event that was difficult, watch it played out by others, and develop new strategies regarding the situation through observation and practice.

Materials needed

Writing materials for note-taking

People needed

Three or more

Procedure

Begin by asking the participant to think about a time that was particularly difficult for her. Inform the participant that she will be asked to share the event or time with the group and only needs to share relevant information for the role play (no names or specific information that could be too difficult). When possible, shape the conversation toward a very specific difficulty that happened in the recent past. Inform the listeners to focus very closely on the details of the story as some of them will be asked to play characters from the tough day.

Once the participant sharing the story is ready to begin, prepare to make an outline of her story with critical details on large paper or some other writing area.

After she has delivered the story and notes have been collected:

1. Determine how many role-players will be needed to re-enact the story.
2. Discuss the outline you have generated and make sure with the participant that the outline reflects the event truthfully.
3. Assign roles to other participants; the storyteller will observe the playback.
4. Have the participants play back the story according to their perception of the events, using the outline to shape the role play if needed.
5. Repeat the role play, if necessary, to refine the events or to include moments the storyteller left out and wants to include.

After the role play has been completed:

1. Ask the original storyteller to discuss how it felt to watch others play out the scenario. Encourage her to make notes on the Activity 1.10: Tough Day Playback form.
2. Ask the original storyteller to discuss moments from the role play that surprised or encouraged her. Encourage her to make notes on the Activity 1.10: Tough Day Playback form.

Next, have the original storyteller join the role play but as a *different character*, not as herself:

1. Ask the original storyteller to discuss how it felt to play out the scenario as someone else. Encourage her to make notes on the Activity 1.10: Tough Day Playback form.
2. Ask the original storyteller to discuss ways she might handle similar situations in the future. Encourage her to make notes on the Activity 1.10: Tough Day Playback form.

ACTIVITY 1.10: TOUGH DAY PLAYBACK

Watching others play out my story made me think/feel…

I was surprised or encouraged when I saw…

When I played someone else in my story, it made me think/feel…

In the future I might…

ACTIVITY 1.11: GOOD DAY PLAYBACK

Purpose

To talk through an event that was positive, watch it played out by others, and assess strengths regarding the situation through observation and practice.

Materials needed

Writing materials for note-taking

People needed

Three or more

Procedure

Begin by asking the participant to think about a time that was particularly exciting or positive for him. Inform the participant that he will be asked to share the event or time with the group and only needs to share relevant information for the role play (no names or specific information that could be uncomfortable). When possible, shape the conversation toward a very specific positive event that happened in the recent past. Inform the listeners to focus very closely on the details of the story as some of them will be asked to play characters from the good day.

Once the participant sharing the story is ready to begin, prepare to make an outline of his story with critical details on large paper or some other writing area.

After he has delivered the story and notes have been collected:

1. Determine how many role-players will be needed to re-enact the story.
2. Discuss the outline you have generated and make sure with the participant that the outline reflects the event truthfully.
3. Assign roles to other participants; the storyteller will observe the playback.
4. Have the participants play back the story according to their perception of the events, using the outline to shape the role play if needed.
5. Repeat the role play, if necessary, to refine the events or to include moments the storyteller left out and wants to include

After the role play has been completed:

1. Ask the original storyteller to discuss how it felt to watch others play out the scenario. Encourage him to make notes on the Activity 1.11: Good Day Playback form.
2. Ask the original storyteller to discuss moments from the role play that surprised or encouraged him. Encourage him to make notes on the Activity 1.11: Good Day Playback form.

Next, ask the original storyteller to join the role play but as a *different character*, not as himself.

1. Ask the original storyteller to discuss how it felt to play out the scenario as someone else. Encourage him to make notes on the Activity 1.11: Good Day Playback form.
2. Ask the original storyteller to discuss ways he might use the positive experience in the future. Encourage him to make notes on the Activity 1.11: Good Day Playback form.

ACTIVITY 1.11: GOOD DAY PLAYBACK

Watching others play out my story made me think/feel…

I was surprised or encouraged when I saw…

When I played someone else in my story, it made me think/feel…

In the future I might…

ACTIVITY 1.12: OUR INTERESTS

Purpose

To take the perspective of others by talking about their interests.

Materials needed

Writing materials

People needed

Two or more

Procedure

Begin by discussing the importance of valuing others' interests, regardless of our knowledge or curiosity about the topic. Describe how others appreciate being listened to and how letting others share their interests without protest is an important social skill.

Following the pre-discussion, ask the participants to complete the top box in the Activity 1.12: Our Interests form about their own interests.

Once the participants have completed the top box on the Activity 1.12: Our Interests form, have them read their sheets to their role-play partner. Then have the participants trade papers and read them again as the other person.

Discuss how it felt to:

1. tell their interests to a partner
2. listen to the interests of their partner
3. read their partner's interests
4. listen to their partner read their personal interests.

Record reactions and thoughts on the Activity 1.12: Our Interests form.

End the role play by trying to help the participants connect to the realization that we all have our own passions, we all want to be heard, and we can give others our attention even when we are not completely excited by the topic they are discussing.

ACTIVITY 1.12: OUR INTERESTS

My interests

My favorite thing to talk about is…

I like this topic or area because…

Three things most people don't know about this topic are…

How it felt to:

1. tell my interests to a partner…

2. listen to the interests of my partner…

3. read my partner's interests…

4. listen to my partner read their personal interests…

How does this apply to me and how I think about others' interests?

ACTIVITY 1.13: MY TURN TO TEACH

Purpose

To develop an awareness of the struggles and successes of being a teacher and what it feels like to teach others.

Materials needed

Chairs, desks if possible, other materials specific to teaching lesson, writing materials

People needed

Three or more

Procedure

Begin by informing the participants that one or more of them will get a chance to teach the others a simple lesson, but that the role play will involve different reactions to their teaching. Get them thinking about a simple skill they would like to teach (tying a shoe, drawing a smiley face, making a paper airplane, for example) and how they will teach the lesson.

Have the participants write their teaching skill/lesson, together with how they will teach that lesson, on the top of the Activity 1.13: My Turn to Teach form.

Then choose one participant to begin teaching the lesson to the other participants as though they were in an actual classroom. Inform the "students" that they will be working in the role play to cooperate enthusiastically, not respond, or talk out during the lesson. Instruct the teacher to begin teaching and the students to begin reacting according to one of the aforementioned "student conditions":

1. cooperating enthusiastically with the lesson
2. not responding to the lesson
3. talking out and interrupting during the lesson.

Take each "teacher" through all three conditions in one role play and then discuss their reactions to the role play. Have them document their thoughts and feelings on the Activity 1.13: My Turn to Teach form.

Then have each participant reflect on times when they have been the student and they were cooperative, non-responsive, or were talking out. Discuss these issues from the perspective of the teacher and document on the Activity 1.13: My Turn to Teach form.

ACTIVITY 1.13: MY TURN TO TEACH

What I want to teach…

Materials I will need…

Simple steps to teach the skill…

When I was the teacher…

Cooperating and enthusiastic students made me feel:

Non-responsive students made me feel:

Talking out or interrupting students made me feel:

Times when I have been cooperative, non-responsive, or talking out…

What can I change to help out my teacher?

ACTIVITY 1.14: JUST AS I AM

Purpose

To empathize with others, embrace others' differences, and embrace what is different within one's self.

Materials needed

Writing materials

People needed

Two or more, some with and some without an ASD diagnosis

Procedure

Begin by having the participants discuss and write down things that make them different from others. It is important to include typical peers as well when possible. Encourage them to explore aspects of themselves such as wearing glasses, having freckles, being tall or short, having asthma or allergies, liking funny foods, having an illness, or having a disability. Encourage the participants to write down their ideas on the Activity 1.14: Just as I Am form. Inform them that you will be collecting the forms and handing them out to others to read.

Assure participants that this will be a safe exercise by establishing the following ground rules:

1. We will uplift and respect one another by listening and participating.
2. We will celebrate one another's differences and encourage others.
3. We will keep our environment safe and free of teasing or bullying.
4. We will treat the information others share with respect and dignity, and will not share information with others without the consent of each role-player.
5. We will accept one another Just As We Are.

Assign each Activity 1.14: Just as I Am form to someone other than the original author. Give a moment for each to look at their new form. Then, one by one, have participants read their new form. End each presentation with applause and celebration.

Finish by discussing reactions to:

1. hearing someone read their form
2. reading someone else's form.

Document reactions on the participants' Activity 1.14: Just as I Am form.

ACTIVITY 1.14: JUST AS I AM

Script

My name is…

You and I have a lot in common. But we are different as well. I have…

So, there are probably some things about me that make me different from you. But we have to remember that we all have at least one thing in common—we all need help from one another to get through life. Please accept me Just as I Am!

Things I learned when reading…

Things I learned when listening to mine being read…

Chapter 2

ROLE PLAY FOR TEACHERS AND CAREGIVERS

Case Study: Katie's Realization in a Specific Behavior Strategy Role Play

During a teacher training session for setting up work-stations we decided to role-play what to do when challenging behaviors occur related to transitioning to and from work areas. I had worked with one of the staff at her school prior to the training and was able to play the role of one of her students to work on Specific Behavior Strategies.

In the spring of that year she had been injured by the student after getting too close during a major upset. He had kicked her while lying on his back and had injured her to the point of needing medical attention.

The role play was set up so that teachers had to work together to develop strategies as I presented new challenging behaviors. We worked slowly in "half time" so teachers could have time to think, analyze, and assess the situation. When the time came for Katie to implement a strategy, she hovered over me as I role-played a major upset while lying on the floor. Slowly, I moved my leg toward her face, just as her student had done three months previous to the training. Katie stopped, sat down, and said, "Okay, I get it now." She came to the conclusion through role play that she needed to try other strategies that might be more effective and that would keep her student and herself safe.

Other teachers were able to offer Katie suggestions and we replayed the scenario to give Katie an opportunity to try some new techniques. She executed new strategies that kept her and the student safe. Instead of getting too close and making stern demands during upsets, Katie used visual supports to help show expectations. She learned what positive behaviors to look for and how to reinforce her student when they were experiencing success. Katie also learned how to build momentum with her student enthusiastically by interspersing difficult tasks between simpler, highly preferred activities. Working in this way with Katie gave her new confidence and permission to practice new skills with her colleagues when future challenges arise.

ACTIVITY 2.1: 100 WAYS TO PRAISE

Purpose

To develop new skills and vocabulary for delivering reinforcement.

Materials needed

Writing materials

People needed

One or more teachers or caregivers

Procedure

Begin a discussion about the importance of reinforcement in all of our lives (a compliment from others, a paycheck, a bonus at work, etc.). Talk about the importance of using reinforcement when interacting with others. Also note our tendency either to forget to reinforce positive behaviors or to use one or two reinforcement statements over and over every time we do reinforce.

Have participants think of as many ways as possible to praise someone, and have them write down each praise statement or behavior that they would feel comfortable using on the Activity 2.1: 100 Ways to Praise form.

Then have them imagine behaviors that they would like to praise with a higher frequency in the students they work with. Document these behaviors on the Activity 2.1: 100 Ways to Praise form.

If other role-players are available, partner participants and practice using praise statements. One participant plays the student and exhibits the range of behaviors, and the teacher or caregiver practices using new praise statements.

Build on new praise skills by having participants pair social reinforcers with their new praise statements (high fives, thumbs up, tickles, etc.).

Also, experiment with going from behavior specific praise statements ("good looking," "excellent sitting in your chair," etc.) to more loose or casual forms of praise while role-playing.

ACTIVITY 2.1: 100 WAYS TO PRAISE

Praise statements that I can use...

Other ways to praise without words...

Specific behaviors I want to reinforce in my students

Behavior 1:

Behavior 2:

Behavior 3:

Behavior 4:

Behavior 5:

Behavior 6:

Additional behaviors:

ACTIVITY 2.2: DEFINITIONS FOR DATA

Purpose

To demonstrate the importance of defining behaviors clearly for data collection, and to help teams generate clear definitions for specific behaviors.

Materials needed

Writing materials

People needed

Two or more; a large group is ideal

Procedure

Start a conversation about data collection, asking participants to name some behaviors or skills they have tracked in the past. Then have the group choose a behavior to simulate and collect data on. As the facilitator, be sure that the group chooses a behavior that is *observable but potentially difficult to definitively record*. Some behaviors that work well for this exercise include head hitting, vocal outbursts, whining, crying, and pinching. *Hint: do not define the behavior as a group before Step 1.*

Step 1

Once you have chosen a behavior to collect data on write it on the Activity 2.2: Definitions for Data form and enlist two volunteers (or one if you, as the facilitator, will demonstrate the behavior) to role-play the behavior.

Step 2

Create a framework for the behavior to occur in (one-to-one instruction, math lesson, or some other teacher–student interaction). Ask the participants to role-play the scenario for about one minute while the observers collect frequency data on the behavior on their Activity 2.2: Definitions for Data form.

> *Example: Sue will be the teacher; Ray will pretend to be the student. Sue, I want you to deliver simple math instructions to Ray (1+1, 2–1), and, Ray, I want you to periodically engage in the behavior. It's okay to try and mix in other similar behaviors. Observers, begin collecting frequency data once Sue delivers an instruction.*

Step 3

Stop the role play after about one minute or so. Ask the observers to tally their frequency data and survey them to get a range of how many tallies the individuals within the group collected (range of 3 to 13).

Step 4

Define the behavior as a group on a large piece of paper or blackboard and then write the definition on the Activity 2.2: Definitions for Data form.

Step 5

Repeat steps 2 and 3. Compare the range of tallies pre-definition and post-definition and discuss. Do we need to modify our definition even more? Does our range reflect a reliable behavior definition? What does the difference in range from pre- to post-definition tell us about the need for clear definitions? Encourage participants to use this role-play strategy in the future when defining behaviors.

ACTIVITY 2.2: DEFINITIONS FOR DATA

Target behavior:

Frequency recording, Role Play 1:

Our group's range, Role Play 1:

Target behavior definition:

Examples:

Non-examples:

Frequency recording, Role Play 2:

Our group's range, Role Play 2:

Do we need to redefine or is our range acceptable?

ACTIVITY 2.3: SPECIFIC BEHAVIOR STRATEGIES

Purpose

To give teachers and caregivers the opportunity to discuss, develop, and practice strategies for handling specific behaviors in a safe, controlled environment before implementing.

Materials needed

Writing materials, environmental objects as needed

People needed

One or more; as many from the student's team as possible

Procedure

Begin the role play with a discussion about the challenges we face as teachers when handling difficult or new behaviors as they occur in the normal course of the day. Explain that role play can be used outside of actual situations to develop and practice strategies that may help when challenging behaviors do occur.

Step 1

Have the team choose one behavior that they would like to focus on for developing new strategies. Write this behavior on the Activity 2.3: Specific Behavior Strategies form.

Step 2

Define the behavior as a group and think of examples and non-examples of that behavior. Document the definition and examples on the Activity 2.3: Specific Behavior Strategies form. See Activity 2.2: Definitions for Data for more ideas.

Step 3

Choose one participant to demonstrate the behavior for the group. Then discuss and document what strategies they are currently using to handle the behavior on the Activity 2.3: Specific Behavior Strategies form.

Step 4

Brainstorm 2–5 new positive strategies that could be used to handle the behavior and document them on the Activity 2.3: Specific Behavior Strategies form. Focus on new behaviors to teach the student that might replace the challenging ones as well.

Step 5

Have one participant role-play the student exhibiting the behavior and have as many teacher-participants try one of the strategies developed by the group. Discuss and repeat the strategy if needed. Have participants make notes on the Activity 2.3: Specific Behavior Strategies form regarding specific ideas or concerns.

Step 6

Repeat until all participants have tried a strategy and feel that they could implement one or all of the strategies with the student.

Step 7

Plan to try new strategies, and plan a date when the team will revisit the strategies to evaluate safety and success.

ACTIVITY 2.3: SPECIFIC BEHAVIOR STRATEGIES

Target behavior:

Target behavior definition:

Examples:

Non-examples:

When the behavior occurs now we usually…

New strategies to try if the challenging behavior occurs:

1.

2.

3.

4.

5.

Positive replacement behaviors to strengthen:

Notes:

Date we will revisit and discuss the strategies: _____

ACTIVITY 2.4: WARNING SIGNS, POSITIVE SIGNS

Purpose

To practice recognizing signs that frequently precipitate challenging behaviors and signs that frequently lead to more positive behaviors.

Materials needed

Writing materials

People needed

One or more; as many from the student's team as possible

Procedure

Discuss the importance of being able to spot small, less intense behaviors that may be precursors to more intense challenging behaviors. Talk about how knowing those signals can influence what you do to support the individual on the spectrum and reduce challenging behaviors. Also discuss the power of recognizing positive signals and positive behaviors in individuals with autism.

On the Activity 2.4: Warning Signs, Positive Signs form, have participants think of someone they work with and document 1–3 challenging behaviors they would like to help reduce/replace. Role-play the behavior in situations that often precede the occurrence of the behavior. Watch for warning signs that indicate that the behavior may begin. Discuss and document these signals on the Activity 2.4: Warning Signs, Positive Signs form.

Partner up participants or have them work in groups. Before role-playing, encourage groups to generate as many proactive strategies they can think of to reduce challenging behaviors when warning signs arise. Then have one participant role-play warning signs and behaviors while other participants role-play trying proactive strategies. Document proactive strategies that may be effective on the Activity 2.4: Warning Signs, Positive Signs form.

Then shift focus to positive signals the person may display when he or she is happy/content and when instruction is likely to be successful. Document these signals on the Activity 2.4: Warning Signs, Positive Signs form. Think about the positive opposite of each challenging behavior (screaming = asking for help, biting = saying "I need a break," interrupting = raising hand, etc.). Then document positive behaviors on the Activity 2.4: Warning Signs, Positive Signs form.

Have the participants role-play reinforcing these positive behaviors: one participant plays the positive signals while other participants reinforce. Finish by documenting strategies on the Activity 2.4: Warning Signs, Positive Signs form.

ACTIVITY 2.4: WARNING SIGNS, POSITIVE SIGNS

Target behaviors I would like to help reduce/replace

1.

Warning signs for this behavior…

Steps I can take when warning signs begin…

2.

Warning signs for this behavior…

Steps I can take when warning signs begin…

3.

Warning signs for this behavior…

Steps I can take when warning signs begin…

Signs indicating happiness/learning readiness are…

What is the positive opposite of each challenging behavior?

How will I reinforce that positive behavior to build momentum?

ACTIVITY 2.5: IN THE ROOM

Purpose

To practice communication strategies which acknowledge and include the individual with autism when speaking to others.

Materials needed

CD tracks 8–10, CD player, writing materials

People needed

One or more

Procedure

Begin a discussion with participants about who we talk to on a frequent basis about our students with autism. Also discuss who we talk to about the individual when he is present in the room. Ask participants to describe if and how they try to involve the individual with autism in those conversations. Finish the initial discussion by asking the participants if they have ever been surprised by what an individual has said or done to indicate they were listening while people conversed about them. Document ideas generated on the Activity 2.5: In the Room form.

Scenarios

Doctor, Fellow Teacher, Parents: Have one participant play the role of the individual with autism. Ask him to move about casually in the space or sit in a chair. Play the CD for In the Room and ask him to listen as each scenario plays (Doctor, Fellow Teacher, Parents). He can continue to walk in the space or sit as each brief scenario plays.

Ask the participant to think of what he would say during each scenario if he was included in the conversation.

Ask the participant to process how it feels to be talked about without being included as the scenarios play out.

Discussion

After the scenarios have concluded, finish by having a discussion about how it feels to be talked about but not included. Reflect on why we might make assumptions about individuals with autism and their need to be included in conversations. Talk about ways we can work to include individuals with autism in our future discussions, meetings, or conversations. Document reactions and strategies on the Activity 2.5: In the Room form.

ACTIVITY 2.5: IN THE ROOM

Who I talk to on a regular basis about individuals with autism…

Who I talk to when the individual with autism is in the room with us…

A time I was surprised by what an individual said or did indicating they were listening…

How it felt during the…

Doctor role play:

Fellow teacher role play:

Parent role play:

Things I can try to include individuals with autism when talking about matters that involve them…

ACTIVITY 2.6: SHAPING

Purpose

To practice and demonstrate the power of positive reinforcement versus punishment to shape behavior.

Materials needed

Writing materials

People needed

Four or more, preferably a large group

Procedure

Begin by asking for two volunteers from the group. Ask volunteers to assume that applause and cheers are very pleasing and reinforcing to them, and that the other participants will use feedback in the form of applause to get them to "do something." Give no further instructions other than that they are to leave the room and wait until someone calls them in.

While the two volunteers wait outside the room, ask the participants to choose something that the volunteers will be "shaped" to do through applause and reinforcement. Suggest something simple like having the volunteers straighten a pile of messy papers or putting the cap on a pen or marker. Explain that applause and cheers should be used in increasing intensity as the volunteer gets closer to the items and task, and that applause has to stop immediately if the volunteer walks away from the items or uses them inappropriately. This is a similar game to "Hot–Cold" except that applause replaces "You're getting warmer" or "You're getting cold." Have one participant time how long it takes the volunteer to complete the simple task. Ask the first volunteer to enter the room and start the role play.

After the first volunteer completes the simple task, write down the time it took to complete the task. Then, for volunteer 2, switch the role play so that only negative comments will be used to shape behavior. No applause will be given at all during the role play. Only phrases like "no," "wrong," or negative sounds will be used every time volunteer 2 walks away from the items or performs the task incorrectly. No positive reinforcement should be used, only negative feedback for mistakes. Have one participant time how long it takes the volunteer to complete the simple task. Ask volunteer 2 to enter the room and start the role play. If volunteer 2 takes three minutes or longer than the first volunteer, stop the role play.

Finish by talking with the group. Ask time-keepers to share time differences for positive versus negative shaping. Discuss what happened when applause went on too long or was started at the wrong time. Discuss how applause changed once the volunteer "mastered" something or made a mistake in the role play. Discuss how it felt, as trainers, to use only negative feedback. Ask volunteers to compare experiences as well. Finish by talking about how this role play will inform future interactions with individuals with autism. Discuss all observations and reactions on the Activity 2.6: Shaping form.

ACTIVITY 2.6: SHAPING

The volunteers will be asked to…

Time it took volunteer 1 with positive feedback…

Time it took volunteer 2 with negative feedback…

What happened when positive reinforcement was given incorrectly…

What happened to applause and enthusiasm as volunteer 1 "mastered" aspects of the task…

What happened to applause and enthusiasm as volunteer 1 made mistakes…

How it felt giving positive feedback versus negative feedback only…

How it felt receiving positive feedback versus negative feedback only…

In the future I will try…

ACTIVITY 2.7: CRISIS PLAN

Purpose

To practice strategies for protecting individuals during a crisis.

Materials needed

Writing materials

People needed

As many from the student's team as possible

Procedure

Begin a discussion with the team about the individual's strengths first. Then steer the discussion to any challenging behaviors the individual exhibits. Remind the team of the proactive strategies that are in place and have worked in the past. Then list the behaviors that pose the most danger to the individual and those around her. Decide as a team how a crisis will be defined and what events will trigger the implementation of the crisis plan. Document details on the Activity 2.7: Crisis Plan form.

Next, figure out as a team what steps will be taken, in sequence, should a crisis occur. Finish by discussing what measures will be taken once the individual is calm and she and those around her are safe. Document details on the Activity 2.7: Crisis Plan form. Use additional sheets if necessary to document the crisis plan.

Role Play

Have one experienced team member role-play as the individual in crisis and other team members role-play as themselves. Test-run the sequence the team developed by asking the role-player to display crisis behaviors safely while the remaining role-players follow the plan they have developed until the individual is calm. Discuss what worked and what needs to be changed. Make changes to the Activity 2.7: Crisis Plan form and retest the sequence as needed until the team feels comfortable with the plan of action.

Finally, conclude the crisis planning by determining if there are any others who need to approve of the plan or others who may need training regarding what strategies the team will implement in a crisis. Set a date to rehearse the sequence and adjust the crisis plan. Add this information to the Activity 2.7: Crisis Plan form.

ACTIVITY 2.7: CRISIS PLAN

The individual is very good at...

In crisis situations the individual may exhibit challenging behaviors including...

Our team is choosing to focus on protecting the individual and others when...

If a crisis occurs after all proactive strategies have been attempted, the team will...

1.

2.

3.

4.

5.

When the crisis ends and the individual and others are safe, the team will...

Others needing crisis plan training...

The date the team will role-play and adjust crisis strategies: _____

ACTIVITY 2.8: SMALL VICTORIES

Purpose

To practice recognizing and expressing the accomplishments of individuals with autism in potentially negative atmospheres.

Materials needed

CD track 11, CD player, writing materials, chairs if needed

People needed

Two or more

Procedure

Begin by discussing our tendencies to focus on challenging behaviors or situations. Ask participants to share a time or environment in which an individual with autism was talked about in strictly negative terms. Discuss how that affected the group or team, and ultimately how that affected the individual with autism. Document ideas and reactions on the Activity 2.8: Small Victories form.

Next, ask for 2–3 participants to volunteer for role playing. Ask participants to think of 3–5 simple accomplishments of someone with autism they support. For example: "He is cheerful" or "She is trying very hard to tie her shoes" or "He is starting to greet his teachers." Have each participant write these simple accomplishments on the Activity 2.8: Small Victories form. Explain that a CD track with a variety of negative statements will play during the role play, and each participant will read or speak the accomplishments they have written over the noise of negativity in three different conditions:

- Have each participant speak accomplishments at random over the noise of negativity.

- Have each participant look at one another and intentionally speak an accomplishment directly to another participant, one at a time.

- Have each participant increase their volume as loud as they can while speaking accomplishments to the onlookers, or to the "world" if no one is observing the role play.

Finish by asking participants to discuss how it felt to share accomplishments of an individual above the noise of negativity. Also, talk about specific places, situations, and times they can use the role-play skills to remind others of the accomplishments of individuals with autism. Document ideas and reactions on the Activity 2.8: Small Victories form.

ACTIVITY 2.8: SMALL VICTORIES

A time or environment where an individual was talked about in strictly negative terms…

How that affected the group or team…

How that affected the individual with autism…

Accomplishments of a specific individual with autism I support…

1.

2.

3.

4.

5.

How it felt to talk above the noise of negativity…

Places, situations, and times I can put this role play into practice…

ACTIVITY 2.9: TEACHING THE HIDDEN CURRICULUM

Purpose

To emphasize the importance of working with students on specific social rules or customs they may not understand.

Materials needed

Writing materials

People needed

Three or more; large group works well

Procedure

1. Start by asking for a volunteer.

2. Ask the volunteer to leave the room.

3. Once the volunteer has left the room, inform the remaining participants that they need to come up with some silly or ridiculous two-step behavior for the volunteer to perform upon returning to the room (example: "Say Jay Leno and hop on one foot").

4. Participants will not tell the volunteer what two-step behavior to do at this point. Set the ground rule that if the person does not perform the behavior within five seconds of entering, the entire room must erupt with laughter and teasing toward the volunteer.

5. Invite the volunteer back into the room. If the volunteer does not perform the silly two-step behavior within five seconds, cue the room to laugh and tease. Send the volunteer back out of the room.

6. Ask the participants to develop a strategy to help cue the volunteer to perform the behavior (peer model, visual support, etc.) and repeat step 5, keeping the five-second rule.

7. If the volunteer accomplishes the two-step behavior within five seconds, have the participants cheer and clap for the volunteer. If the volunteer fails, reconsider how to teach the two-step behavior and give the volunteer additional support.

8. Repeat step 5. Once the volunteer has accomplished the behavior and the participants have cheered and clapped, facilitate a discussion.

Ask participants why they were asked to choose a silly behavior. Explain that for some individuals on the autism spectrum, social rules and customs can be just as foreign or silly. Also explain that missing these rules can have tremendous social consequences. Then refer back to the role play and emphasize the importance of providing supports and direct teaching of social skills to individuals on the autism spectrum. Encourage participants to consider their own students, current hidden curriculum issues they are facing, and how they might increase support to help their students grasp confusing social rules and customs. Also ask participants to think about the social implications if the student does not receive support for their particular hidden curriculum issues. Document these on the Activity 1: Teaching the Hidden Curriculum form.

ACTIVITY 2.9: TEACHING THE HIDDEN CURRICULUM

What hidden curriculum issues does my student face?

What supports might help this student develop further social understanding?

What are the implications for the individual if these social rules or customs are missed?

ACTIVITY 2.10: WORDS, WORDS, WORDS

Purpose

To simplify instructions and feedback used with individuals with ASD.

Materials needed

CD tracks 12–14, CD player, writing materials

People needed

Two or more

Procedure

Begin a discussion about the emphasis we often place on verbal feedback and how this may cause problems when working with some individuals with ASD. Ask role-play participants to describe a time when they used too much verbal feedback with a student or child. Also ask them to describe a time when they were able to communicate meaningfully with a student or child using no words at all. Record notes on the Activity 2.10: Words, Words, Words form. Determine who will play the role of the student and then play the CD for each condition below.

Track 12, Instructions

As the person role-playing the student listens to this particular track, he must do his best to execute the chain of instructions given on the CD. Following the exercise, have a discussion about the role play, and document notes on the Activity 2.10: Words, Words, Words form.

Track 13, Corrections

As the person role-playing the student listens to this particular track, she must do her best to execute the chain of instructions and make the suggested correction given on the CD. Following the exercise, have a discussion about the role play and document notes on the Activity 2.10: Words, Words, Words form.

Track 14, Feedback

As the person role-playing the student listens to this particular track, he must do his best to remember three key points given in the feedback on the CD. When the track ends, the participant must retell three or more key points from the feedback to the whole group. Following the exercise, have a discussion about the role play, and document notes on the Activity 2.10: Words, Words, Words form.

Note: For training purposes the examples on the CD are accentuated and embellished beyond what most caregivers demonstrate when working with individuals with ASD.

ACTIVITY 2.10: WORDS, WORDS, WORDS

A time I used too many words:

A time I was able to communicate using no words at all:

Track 12, Instructions

Problem:

Future solutions:

Track 13, Corrections

Problem:

Future solutions:

Track 14, Feedback

Three or more key points:

How to simplify:

ACTIVITY 2.11: IT'S AN AUDITORY PROCESS—SCHOOL

Purpose

To develop an awareness of auditory processing issues and to modify interaction strategies for individuals with ASD.

Materials needed

CD tracks 15–17, CD player, writing materials

People needed

One or more

Procedure

Begin by discussing auditory processing issues as they relate to ASD. Use supplementary materials to describe auditory processing disorder to those who may not be familiar with the term. Ask participants to share any personal experiences they may have had with students with processing delays. Then choose a participant to play the role of the student. Play the CD for each scenario, or generate your own scripts to role-play the scenarios. Document how it felt to try to respond in the role play for each scenario on the Activity 2.11: It's an Auditory Process—School form.

1. Track 15, Echo
2. Track 16, Delay
3. Track 17, Script with no delays or issues

Then facilitate a discussion about how we, as teachers, can make adjustments to the environment to support individuals with auditory processing issues, and document tips and strategies on the Activity 2.11: It's an Auditory Process—School form.

ACTIVITY 2.11: IT'S AN AUDITORY PROCESS—SCHOOL

My experiences with auditory processing issues

My reactions to the role-play scenarios

Echo:

Delay:

Script with no delays or issues:

Adjustments I can make in my teaching

ACTIVITY 2.12: THE OTHER 16 HOURS

Purpose

To open dialog between home and school, and to begin a cooperative appreciation for the issues parents and teachers face. Use this exercise in conjunction with The Other Eight Hours.

Materials needed

Writing materials

People needed

Two or more, ideally a mix of an individual's parents and teachers

Procedure

Teamwork and team-building is essential to successful support of individuals with ASD. Collaboration between home and school is critical. Sometimes a lack of understanding of the issues faced in each environment can lead to tension and miscommunication. This role play is designed to allow each team member to develop an understanding of the issues faced by an individual with ASD across environments, and to work as a group to develop new support strategies. Special care should be given during facilitation to promote respect and avoid arguments.

Step 1

Have parents complete the first section of the Activity 2.12: The Other 16 Hours form by writing down specific issues they face in the home.

Step 2

Assign roles for the role play. A parent should play the role of the child, as he or she knows the specific issues and how to role-play them. Have one teacher play the role of the parent. Set the scene with any props or specific information the players will need.

Step 3

Role-play as many scenarios from the Activity 2.12: The Other 16 Hours form as possible.

Step 4

Discuss the role-play scenarios. Talk as a group about discoveries, questions, or ideas that came up during the role play and document on the Activity 2.12: The Other 16 Hours form.

Step 5

If parents want suggestions, discuss the issues as a team and work to develop potential strategies for the issues faced at home. Document on the Activity 2.12: The Other 16 Hours form.

ACTIVITY 2.12: THE OTHER 16 HOURS

Parents document specific issues faced at home

1.

2.

3.

4.

Discoveries about home during the role-play scenarios

Potential home strategies developed by the team

ACTIVITY 2.13: TOUGH DAY PLAYBACK

Purpose

To talk through an event that was difficult, watch it played out by others, and develop new strategies regarding the situation through observation and practice.

Materials needed

Writing materials for note-taking

People needed

Three or more

Procedure

Begin by asking the participant to think about a time that was particularly difficult for her. Inform the participant that she will be asked to share the event or time with the group and only needs to share relevant information for the role play (no names or specific information that could be too difficult). When possible, shape the conversation toward a very specific difficulty that happened in the recent past. Inform the listeners to focus very closely on the details of the story as some of them will be asked to play characters from the tough day.

Once the participant sharing the story is ready to begin, prepare to make an outline of her story with critical details on large paper or some other writing area.

After she has delivered the story and notes have been collected:

1. Determine how many role-players will be needed to re-enact the story.

2. Discuss the outline you have generated and make sure with the participant that the outline reflects the event truthfully.

3. Assign roles to other participants; the storyteller will observe the playback.

4. Have the participants play back the story according to their perception of the events, using the outline to shape the role play if needed.

5. Repeat the role play if necessary to refine the events or to include moments the storyteller left out and wants to include.

After the role play has been completed:

1. Ask the original storyteller to discuss how it felt to watch others play out the scenario. Encourage her to make notes on the Activity 2.13: Tough Day Playback form.

2. Ask the original storyteller to discuss moments from the role play that surprised or encouraged them. Encourage them to make notes on the Activity 2.13: Tough Day Playback form.

Next, have the original storyteller join the role play but as a different character, not as herself.

1. Ask the original storyteller to discuss how it felt to play out the scenario as someone else. Encourage her to make notes on the Activity 2.13: Tough Day Playback form.

2. Ask the original storyteller to discuss ways she might handle similar situations in the future. Encourage her to make notes on the Activity 2.13: Tough Day Playback form.

ACTIVITY 2.13: TOUGH DAY PLAYBACK

Watching others play out my story made me think/feel...

I was surprised or encouraged when I saw...

When I played someone else in my story, it made me think/feel...

In the future I might...

ACTIVITY 2.14: GOOD DAY PLAYBACK

Purpose

To talk through an event that was positive, watch it played out by others, and assess strengths regarding the situation through observation and practice.

Materials needed

Writing materials for note-taking

People needed

Three or more

Procedure

Begin by asking the participant to think about a time that was particularly exciting or positive for him. Inform the participant that he will be asked to share the event or time with the group and only needs to share relevant information for the role play (no names or specific information that could be uncomfortable). When possible, shape the conversation toward a very specific positive event that happened in the recent past. Inform the listeners to focus very closely on the details of the story as some of them will be asked to play characters from the good day.

Once the participant sharing the story is ready to begin, prepare to make an outline of his story with critical details on large paper or some other writing area.

After he has delivered the story and notes have been collected:

1. Determine how many role-players will be needed to re-enact the story.

2. Discuss the outline you have generated and make sure with the participant that the outline reflects the event truthfully.

3. Assign roles to other participants; the storyteller will observe the playback.

4. Have the participants play back the story according to their perception of the events, using the outline to shape the role play if needed.

5. Repeat the role play if necessary to refine the events or to include moments the storyteller left out and wants to include.

After the role play has been completed:

1. Ask the original storyteller to discuss how it felt to watch others play out the scenario. Encourage him to make notes on the Activity 2.14: Good Day Playback form.

2. Ask the original storyteller to discuss moments from the role play that surprised or encouraged him. Encourage him to make notes on the Activity 2.14: Good Day Playback form.

Next, ask the original storyteller to join the role play but as a different character, not as himself:

1. Ask the original storyteller to discuss how it felt to play out the scenario as someone else. Encourage him to make notes on the Activity 2.14: Good Day Playback form.

2. Ask the original storyteller to discuss ways he might use the positive experience in the future. Encourage him to make notes on the Activity 2.14: Good Day Playback form.

ACTIVITY 2.14: GOOD DAY PLAYBACK

> Watching others play out my story made me think/feel…

> I was surprised or encouraged when I saw…

> When I played someone else in my story, it made me think/feel…

> In the future I might…

ACTIVITY 2.15: PUSH-PULL

Purpose

To use physical-vocal exploration to examine the barriers impeding independence.

Materials needed

Bright tape or a rope, writing materials

People needed

Two or more

Procedure

Begin by discussing the issue of independence for individuals with autism. What are the natural barriers in society and the environment? What are common social or behavioral barriers to independence? Then begin to discuss limitations we as teachers have placed on the individual based on our fears or beliefs. Document these ideas on the Activity 2.15: Push-Pull form. Next, take a bright piece of tape or rope and place it in the room in an area with enough room for movement. This line will become the line between dependence and independence. Describe to the participants that they will be gently pushing and pulling their partner from that line of independence.

1. Practice gently pulling and pushing your role-playing partner in the space. Develop a comfortable and controlled physical interaction style. One person will role-play the individual with autism and others will role-play as caregivers.

2. Begin by asking the caregiver(s) to imagine a time when she limited an individual's independence and to give the moment a simple sentence: for example, "I was afraid they would fail." Ask her to develop a simple sentence that reflects the independence the person with autism was trying to achieve: for example, "I want to live on my own." Document these ideas on the Activity 2.15: Push-Pull form.

3. Have the participant playing the individual with autism start walking toward the tape or rope line, and the participant playing the caregiver gently pull her partner back from the line. Also have the pulling participant imagine, but not speak, the simple sentence she generated in step 2.

4. Repeat the above process. This time ask the participant playing the caregiver to speak her simple sentence as she pulls her role-playing partner back from the line. Also ask the participant playing the individual with autism to speak her simple sentence of independence.

5. Repeat this sequence 3–5 times in fluid and continuous loops so the caregiver participant pulls and verbalizes her fear and the participant playing the individual with autism verbalizes her sentence of independence several times.

6. Stop and discuss the role play and strategies for the future to promote and encourage independence. Document these ideas on the Activity 2.15: Push-Pull form.

ACTIVITY 2.15: PUSH-PULL

Some common societal or environmental barriers to independence are…

Some common social or behavioral barriers to independence are…

Some ways my fears or beliefs have limited an individual's independence…

Barrier sentences that might describe my fear or belief ("What If They Fail?")…

Sentences that describe what independence the individual with autism was working to achieve ("I Want To Live On My Own")…

How I can change my thoughts or actions to encourage an individual's independence in the future…

ACTIVITY 2.16: THE STRANGER

Purpose

To experience foreign social customs or behaviors and to empathize with those who may struggle to decode our social world.

Materials needed

Writing materials

People needed

Between 3 and 15

Procedure

Begin by having one participant volunteer to play the role of the stranger. Ask the participant to leave the room until the other participants have finished preparing for the rest of the role play. Inform him that you will cue him when it is time to return. Also, instruct him that when he does return all he is asked to do is interact with his peers normally. Next, work with the remaining group to develop 2–3 customs that the "stranger" would have no way of knowing. Explain that these customs should be simple, yet quite different from "everyday behavior." Help the group discover customs using the following guidelines:

1. A strange language

The group (minus the stranger) should develop a simple language to use as a group. For example, the group could speak only in verbs, use sounds only, or speak only in adjectives. Have the group practice speaking in their new, strange language and document the language specifics on the Activity 2.16: The Stranger form.

2. Strange physical behavior

The group should also develop a few strange non-verbal, physical behaviors. For example, the group could blink excessively or pull on their ears anytime they begin speaking. Have the group practice speaking in their new, strange language and using strange physical behaviors. Document the behavior specifics on the Activity 2.16: The Stranger form.

3. Laughing at something the stranger does

Help the group choose something simple the stranger may do to laugh at during the role play. For example, the group may choose to laugh whenever the stranger takes a step, sits down, speaks or gestures. Have the group practice speaking in their strange language, using strange physical behaviors, and preparing to laugh at the stranger. Document which behavior the group will laugh at on the Activity 2.16: The Stranger form.

Prepare the group and have the participant role-playing the stranger return to the space. Let the role play unfold for 3–10 minutes. Stop the role play at a natural place. Discuss reactions on the part of the stranger to the way the role play felt and what sort of conclusions he tried to make as the scenario unfolded. Relate these conclusions to how an individual on the autism spectrum may feel in the actual social realm. Also, discuss the reactions of the group as to how it felt to exclude someone, talk around them, and ignore their confusion. Document all reactions on the Activity 2.16: The Stranger form.

ACTIVITY 2.16: THE STRANGER

Our strange language…

Our strange physical behavior(s)…

We will laugh when the stranger…

The role play made the participant playing the stranger feel…

How this might relate to an individual on the autism spectrum…

Playing a member of the large group made me feel…

ACTIVITY 2.17: MY STUDENT'S DREAM

Purpose

To identify with an individual's dream and develop ideas to support that dream.

Materials needed

Writing materials

People needed

One or more

Procedure

Begin talking with the participant(s) about their student. Discuss her interests and strengths, things she talks about often or does particularly well. Ask the participant(s) to begin to walk in the shoes of the student. Encourage each participant to think about what sort of career their student would like to pursue, where she would prefer to live, places she dreams of visiting, or achievements she seeks. Have each participant reflect to ensure they are dreaming *as* the student and not *for* the student, and document discoveries on the Activity 2.17: My Student's Dream form.

Next, have the participants choose a handful of details from their student's dreams to role-play. Have them choose a career, an achievement, a quote, or sentences that the student may say in her life, and an action that represents one or more of those dreams. For example, the student may dream of accepting the Nobel Prize. The role-playing participant could walk from the audience to the podium, receive the award, and say a few words of thanks. Encourage participants to look at their notes to find actions, words, and emotions from their student's dream to role-play and begin.

After the participants have played one or more moments from their student's dream, have them reflect on how it felt to say, do, and feel something as their student. Document reactions on the Activity 2.17: My Student's Dream form.

Conclude by asking participants to think of ways they can discuss future dreams with their students and how they can support their student in the pursuit of those dreams. Document strategies and ideas on the Activity 2.17: My Student's Dream form.

ACTIVITY 2.17: MY STUDENT'S DREAM

My student dreams of being a…

My student dreams of living…

My student dreams of seeing/doing…

…I believe these are their dreams, not my dreams for them.

Saying, doing, and feeling something as my student made me realize…

I can help foster my student's dreams by…

Chapter 3

ROLE PLAY FOR PARENTS

Case Study: James and Cindy's Parent-Guided Role Plays

James and Cindy were parents to Karl, a four-year-old boy with autism. Karl was incredibly smart and was reading well above grade level and developing new communication skills at a rapid rate. James and Cindy were interested in creative ways to teach Karl social skills such as play, sharing, handling change, and preparing for trips into the community.

We introduced the idea of role play with Karl by beginning with a scenario to help teach him how to modulate his voice volume in various social situations. He was fascinated with animals, so we assigned an animal to each volume level (mouse is quiet, penguin is normal, lion is loud, etc.). Karl's parents experimented with role-playing different social scenarios where they were able to cue various animal voices to help him learn when to use which volume level.

James and Cindy enjoyed working with Karl in this playful way so we introduced new role plays such as Stranger Safety and A Trip to The... proactively to help Karl prepare for life situations in as many ways as possible before challenges developed.

Karl's self-advocacy and emotional self-reliance, even at four years old, has developed tremendously due to his parents' willingness to practice and role-play what to say and do in a variety of situations. James and Cindy did not feel silly, or at least overcame inhibitions very quickly when it came to playing with Karl in this new way. They are a convincing example of the powerful creativity and fun that role play brings when teaching new skills and perspectives to children in the home environment.

ACTIVITY 3.1: IEP DAY

Purpose

To prepare for the demands of an IEP or similar planning meeting.

Materials needed

Writing materials, tables, chairs

People needed

Three or more; other parents with IEP experience if needed

Procedure

Begin by having a conversation about the participants' experience with IEP meetings. Discuss how meetings can be stressful, and how preparation and practice can help to ensure a meeting where all concerns and ideas are shared. Set clear expectations that the role play is designed to practice for the meeting. Personal issues with school or service personnel should be avoided or handled with respect in the role play.

Step 1

Have parents complete the top section regarding meeting concerns, ideas, goals, and questions they want to address on the Activity 3.1: IEP Day form.

Step 2

Identify and assign roles for the role play based on likely meeting attendees. Parents should play the role of parents when possible. Work carefully to ensure that role-players play the "general role" of principal or case manager and avoid the use of caricatures of actual meeting attendees.

Step 3

Begin role-playing an actual IEP or similar meeting. Go through the actions of signing documents, greeting one another, working through the IEP or meeting topic, just as the meeting will be conducted. Help parents by encouraging them to work through the points they have written on the Activity 3.1: IEP Day form. Do your best as a role-playing team to let the role play be as authentic and honest as possible.

Step 4

As a group, discuss the role play. Ask if the parents felt that they accomplished their goals. Discuss tips the parents will need to remember going into the actual meeting, and document on the Activity 3.1: IEP Day form.

ACTIVITY 3.1: IEP DAY

My concerns for this meeting are…

I want to be sure to address these specific issues, goals, questions:

1.

2.

3.

4.

5.

6.

Other issues:

I know I will need to…

…to feel comfortable, confident, and successful.

ACTIVITY 3.2: A TRIP TO THE...

Purpose

To prepare an individual, group, or family for an outing by practicing skills and rehearsing expectations before the event or trip.

Materials needed

Props that mirror the anticipated environment if necessary, writing materials

People needed

Two or more; as many from the group going on the outing as possible

Procedure

We all rehearse responses before events take place (Ramamoorthi 2008), and practice in our minds what we will say and do in particular situations before they occur. Sometimes this kind of planning is difficult for individuals on the autism spectrum. Begin a discussion with the parents about times when they have gone somewhere and have had unexpected challenges develop for their son or daughter. Talk about what kind of preparation work they had done and what things they could have prepared for before leaving.

Step 1

Ask the participants to think of either a real event or outing coming up for their family or an event that might happen some time in the future (dentist visit, haircut, wedding, road trip, etc.). Have them choose one outing or event to work on for this particular role play and document it on the Activity 3.2: A Trip to The... form.

Step 2

Have the participants list the major steps involved in going to this outing on the Activity 3.2: A Trip to The...form. Discuss any props needed. Let the individual with autism know that you are preparing for the specific event and will be pretending to do some of the things associated with the event with him.

Step 4

Assign roles to the group members supporting the individual with ASD (waiter, bus driver, dentist, etc.) and have them role-play the sequence of steps they have listed on the Activity 3.2: A Trip to The... form. Ask the individual with autism to role play as himself.

Step 4

Discuss the role play as a group and make notes and changes on the Activity 3.2: A Trip to The... form. Also, have participants document specific times and dates when they will do the role play again before going on the outing.

ACTIVITY 3.2: A TRIP TO THE...

Outing/event _____

The major steps involved in executing this outing...

1.

2.

3.

4.

5.

6.

7.

8.

9.

10.

Props needed:

Notes or changes to be made to the role play...

Date we will practice this event sequence again on: _____

ACTIVITY 3.3: 100 WAYS TO PRAISE

Purpose

To develop new skills and vocabulary for delivering reinforcement.

Materials needed

Writing materials

People needed

One or more parents or caregivers

Procedure

Begin a discussion about the importance of reinforcement in all of our lives (a compliment from others, a paycheck, a bonus at work, etc.). Talk about the importance of using reinforcement when interacting with others. Also note our tendency to either forget to reinforce positive behaviors or to use one or two reinforcement statements over and over every time we do reinforce.

Have participants think of as many ways to praise someone as possible and have them write down each praise statement that they would feel comfortable using on the Activity 3.3: 100 Ways to Praise form.

Then have them imagine behaviors that they would like to praise with a higher frequency in their children. Document these behaviors on the Activity 3.3: 100 Ways to Praise form.

If other role-players are available, partner participants and practice using praise statements. One participant plays the child and exhibits the range of behaviors, and the parent or caregiver practices using new praise statements.

Build on new praise skills by having participants pair social reinforcers with their new praise statements (high fives, thumbs up, tickles, etc.).

Also, experiment with going from behavior specific praise statements ("good looking," "excellent sitting in your chair," etc.) to more loose or casual forms of praise while role-playing.

ACTIVITY 3.3: 100 WAYS TO PRAISE

Praise statements that I can use…

Specific behaviors I want to reinforce in my child

Behavior 1:

Behavior 2:

Behavior 3:

Behavior 4:

Behavior 5:

Behavior 6:

Additional behaviors:

ACTIVITY 3.4: WARNING SIGNS, POSITIVE SIGNS

Purpose

To practice recognizing signs that frequently precipitate challenging behaviors and signs that frequently lead to more positive behaviors.

Materials needed

Writing materials

People needed

One or more; as many from the child's life as possible

Procedure

Discuss the importance of being able to spot small, less intense behaviors that may be precursors to more intense challenging behaviors. Talk about how knowing those signals can influence what you do to support the individual on the spectrum and reduce challenging behaviors. Also discuss the power of recognizing positive signals and positive behaviors in individuals with autism.

On the Activity 3.4: Warning Signs, Positive Signs form have participants think about their child and document 1–3 challenging behaviors they would like to help reduce/replace. Role-play the behavior in situations that often precede the occurrence of the behavior. Watch for warning signs that indicate the behavior may begin. Discuss and document these signals on the Activity 3.4: Warning Signs, Positive Signs form.

Partner-up participants or have them work in groups. Before role-playing, encourage groups to generate as many proactive strategies they can think of to reduce challenging behaviors when warning signs arise. Then have one participant role-play warning signs and behaviors while other participants role-play trying proactive strategies. Document proactive strategies that may be effective on the Activity 3.4: Warning Signs, Positive Signs form.

Then shift focus to positive signals the person may display when he or she is happy/content and when instruction is likely to be successful. Document these signals on the Activity 3.4: Warning Signs, Positive Signs form. Think about the positive opposite of each challenging behavior (screaming = asking for help, biting = saying "I need a break," interrupting = raising hand, etc.). Then document positive behaviors on the Activity 3.4: Warning Signs, Positive Signs form.

Have the participants role-play reinforcing these positive behaviors. One participant plays the positive signals while other participants reinforce. Finish by documenting strategies on the Activity 3.4: Warning Signs, Positive Signs form.

ACTIVITY 3.4: WARNING SIGNS, POSITIVE SIGNS

Target behaviors I would like to help reduce/replace

1.

Warning signs for this behavior…

Steps I can take when warning signs begin…

2.

Warning signs for this behavior…

Steps I can take when warning signs begin…

3.

Warning signs for this behavior…

Steps I can take when warning signs begin…

Signs indicating happiness/learning readiness are…

What is the positive opposite of each challenging behavior?

How will I reinforce that positive behavior to build momentum?

ACTIVITY 3.5: SPECIFIC BEHAVIOR STRATEGIES

Purpose

To give parents the opportunity to develop and practice strategies for handling specific behaviors in a safe environment before implementing.

Materials needed

Writing materials, environmental objects as needed

People needed

One or more; as many from the child's team as possible

Procedure

Begin the role play with a discussion about the challenges we face as parents when handling difficult or new behaviors as they occur in the normal course of the day. Explain that role play can be used outside of actual situations to develop and practice strategies that may help when challenging behaviors do occur.

Step 1

Have the team choose one behavior that they would like to focus on for developing new strategies. Write this behavior on the Activity 3.5: Specific Behavior Strategies form.

Step 2

Define the behavior as a group and think of examples and non-examples of that behavior. Document the definition and examples on the Activity 3.5: Specific Behavior Strategies form. See Teachers, Developing Skills Activity 2.2: Definitions for Data for more ideas.

Step 3

Choose one participant to demonstrate the behavior for the group. Then discuss and document what strategies are currently being used to handle the behavior on the Activity 3.5: Specific Behavior Strategies form.

Step 4

Brainstorm 2–5 new positive strategies that could be used to handle the behavior and document them on the Activity 3.5: Specific Behavior Strategies form. Focus on new behaviors to teach the child that might replace the challenging ones as well.

Step 5

Have one participant role-play the child exhibiting the behavior, and have as many parents and team members try one of the strategies developed by the group. Discuss and repeat the strategy if needed. Have participants make notes on the Activity 3.5: Specific Behavior Strategies form regarding specific ideas or concerns.

Step 6

Repeat until all participants have tried a strategy and feel that they could implement one or all of the strategies with the child.

Step 7

Plan to try new strategies and plan a date when the team will revisit the strategies to evaluate safety and success.

ACTIVITY 3.5: SPECIFIC BEHAVIOR STRATEGIES

Target behavior:

Target behavior definition:

Examples:

Non-examples:

When the behavior occurs now, we usually…

New strategies to try if the challenging behavior occurs:

1.

2.

3.

4.

5.

Positive replacement behaviors to strengthen:

Notes:

Date we will revisit and discuss the strategies: _____

ACTIVITY 3.6: IN THE ROOM

Purpose

To practice communication strategies which acknowledge and include the individual with autism when speaking to others.

Materials needed

CD tracks 18–20, CD player, writing materials

People needed

One or more

Procedure

Begin a discussion with participants about who we talk to on a frequent basis about our students with autism. Also discuss who we talk to about the individual when he is present in the room. Ask participants to describe if and how they try to involve the individual with autism in those conversations. Finish the initial discussion by asking the participants if they have ever been surprised by what an individual has said or done to indicate he was listening while people conversed about him. Document ideas generated on the Activity 3.6: In the Room form.

Scenarios – Doctor, Teachers, Parents

Have one participant play the role of the individual with autism. Ask him to move about casually in the space or sit in a chair. Play the CD tracks for In the Room and ask him to listen as each scenario plays. He can continue to walk in the space or sit as each brief scenario plays.

Ask the participant to think of what he would say during each scenario if he was included in the conversation.

Ask the participant to process how it feels to be talked about without being included as the scenarios play out.

Discussion

After the scenarios have concluded, finish by having a discussion about how it feels to be talked about but not included. Reflect on why we might make assumptions about individuals with autism and their need to be included in conversations. Talk about ways we can work to include individuals with autism in our future discussions, meetings, or conversations. Document reactions and strategies on the Activity 3.6: In the Room form.

ACTIVITY 3.6: IN THE ROOM

Who I talk to on a regular basis about individuals with autism…

Who I talk to when the individual with autism is in the room with us…

A time I was surprised by what an individual said or did indicating they were listening…

How it felt during the…

Doctor role play

Teacher role play

Parent role play

Things I can try to include individuals with autism when talking about matters that involve them…

ACTIVITY 3.7: SHAPING

Purpose

To practice and demonstrate the power of positive reinforcement versus punishment to shape behavior.

Materials needed

Writing materials

People needed

Four or more, preferably a large group

Procedure

Begin by asking for two volunteers from the group. Ask volunteers to assume that applause and cheers are very pleasing and reinforcing to them and that the other participants will use feedback in the form of applause to get them to "do something." Give no further instructions other than that they are to leave the room and wait until someone calls them in.

While the two volunteers wait outside the room, ask the participants to choose something that the volunteers will be "shaped" to do through applause and reinforcement. Suggest something simple like having the volunteers straighten a pile of messy papers or putting the cap on a pen or marker. Explain that applause and cheers should be used in increasing intensity as the volunteer gets closer to the items and task, and that applause has to stop immediately if the volunteer walks away from the items or uses them inappropriately. This is a similar game to "Hot–Cold" except that applause replaces "You're getting warmer" or "You're getting cold." Have one participant time how long it takes the volunteer to complete the simple task. Ask the first volunteer to enter the room and start the role play.

After the first volunteer completes the simple task, write down the time it took to complete the task. Then, for volunteer 2, switch the role play so that only negative comments will be used to shape behavior. No applause will be given at all during the role play. Only phrases like "no," "wrong," or negative sounds will be used every time volunteer 2 walks away from the items or performs the task incorrectly. No positive reinforcement should be used, only negative feedback for mistakes. Have one participant time how long it takes the volunteer to complete the simple task. Ask volunteer 2 to enter the room and start the role play. If volunteer 2 takes three minutes or longer than the first volunteer, stop the role play.

Finish by talking with the group. Ask time-keepers to share time differences for positive versus negative shaping. Discuss what happened when applause went on too long or was started at the wrong time. Discuss how applause changed once the volunteer "mastered" something or made a mistake in the role play. Discuss how it felt, as trainers, to use only negative feedback. Ask volunteers to compare experiences as well. Finish by talking about how this role play will inform future interactions with individuals with autism. Discuss all observations and reactions on the Activity 3.7: Shaping form.

ACTIVITY 3.7: SHAPING

The volunteers will be asked to…

Time it took volunteer 1 with positive feedback…

Time it took volunteer 2 with negative feedback…

What happened when positive reinforcement was given incorrectly…

What happened to applause and enthusiasm as volunteer 1 "mastered" aspects of the task…

What happened to applause and enthusiasm as volunteer 1 made mistakes…

How it felt giving positive feedback only…

How it felt receiving positive feedback only…

In the future I will try…

ACTIVITY 3.8: CRISIS PLAN

Purpose

To practice strategies for protecting individuals during a crisis.

Materials needed

Writing materials

People needed

As many from the individual's team as possible

Procedure

Begin a discussion with the team about the individual's strengths first. Then steer the discussion to any challenging behaviors the individual exhibits. Remind the team of the proactive strategies that are in place and have worked in the past. Then list the behaviors that pose the most danger to the individual and those around her. Decide as a team how a crisis will be defined and what events will trigger the implementation of the crisis plan. Document details on the Activity 3.8: Crisis Plan form.

Next, figure out as a team what steps will be taken, in sequence, should a crisis occur. Finish by discussing what measures will be taken once the individual is calm and she and those around them are safe. Document details on the Activity 3.8: Crisis Plan form. Use additional sheets if necessary to document the crisis plan.

Role play

Have one experienced team member role-play as the individual in crisis and other team members role-play as themselves. Test-run the sequence the team developed by asking the role-player to display crisis behaviors safely while the remaining role-players follow the plan they have developed until the individual is calm. Discuss what worked and what needs to be changed. Make changes to the Activity 3.8: Crisis Plan form and retest the sequence as needed until the team feels comfortable with the plan of action.

Finally, conclude the crisis planning by determining if there are any others who need to approve of the plan or others who may need training regarding what strategies the team will implement in a crisis. Set a date to rehearse the sequence and adjust the crisis plan. Add this information to the Activity 3.8: Crisis Plan form.

ACTIVITY 3.8: CRISIS PLAN

The individual is very good at...

In crisis situations the individual may exhibit challenging behaviors including...

Our team is choosing to focus on protecting the individual and others when...

If a crisis occurs after all proactive strategies have been attempted, the team will...

1.

2.

3.

4.

5.

When the crisis ends and the individual and others are safe, the team will...

Others needing crisis plan training...

The date the team will role-play and adjust crisis strategies: _____

ACTIVITY 3.9: SMALL VICTORIES

Purpose

To practice recognizing and expressing the accomplishments of individuals with autism in potentially negative atmospheres.

Materials needed

CD track 21, CD player, writing materials, chairs if needed

People needed

Two or more

Procedure

Begin by discussing our tendencies to focus on challenging behaviors or situations. Ask participants to share a time or environment in which an individual with autism was talked about in strictly negative terms. Discuss how that affected the group or team, and ultimately how that affected the individual with autism. Document ideas and reactions on the Activity 3.9: Small Victories form.

Next, ask for 2–3 participants to volunteer for role playing. Ask each participant to think of 3–5 simple accomplishments of someone with autism they support. For example: "He is cheerful," or "She is trying very hard to tie her shoes," or "he is starting to greet his teachers." Have each participant write these simple accomplishments on the Activity 3.9: Small Victories form. Explain that a CD track with a variety of negative statements will play during the role play and each participant will read or speak the accomplishments they have written over the noise of negativity in three different conditions:

- Have each participant speak accomplishments at random over the noise of negativity.

- Have each participant look at one another and intentionally speak an accomplishment directly to another participant, one at a time.

- Have each participant increase their volume as loud as they can while speaking accomplishments to the onlookers, or to the "world" if no one is observing the role play.

Finish by asking participants to discuss how it felt to share accomplishments of an individual above the noise of negativity. Also, talk about specific places, situations, and times they can use the role-play skills to remind others of the accomplishments of individuals with autism. Document ideas and reactions on the Activity 3.9: Small Victories form.

ACTIVITY 3.9: SMALL VICTORIES

A time or environment where an individual was talked about in strictly negative terms…

How that affected the group or team…

How that affected the individual with autism…

Accomplishments of a specific individual with autism I support…

1.

2.

3.

4.

5.

How it felt to talk above the noise of negativity…

Places, situations, and times I can put this role play into practice…

ACTIVITY 3.10: STRESS RELIEF

Purpose

To identify and practice specific stress-relieving strategies.

Materials needed

Writing materials

People needed

Two or more

Procedure

Begin a general discussion about stress. Ask participants to talk about how stress affects their lives and family. Using the Activity 3.10: Stress Relief form, have participants list as many of their specific stressors as possible in the categories Minimally, Moderately, and Extremely stressful.

Next, discuss with participants strategies they currently use to reduce stress successfully. Ask when, where, and how questions to illuminate what it is about each strategy that makes it successful. Document these ideas on the Activity 3.10: Stress Relief form.

Then, have participants choose four stressors from their list that they would like to develop strategies for. Write these stressors on the Activity 3.10: Stress Relief form. Form partner groups and brainstorm specific strategies for each of the four stressors.

Role-play each condition by having one partner play out the stressful behavior or situation while the primary partner attempts to implement the new stress-relieving strategy. Take notes on what felt good, what needs to be changed, and what aspects of the strategies were successful. Document the final version of each strategy on the Activity 3.10: Stress Relief form.

Ensure that each participant has had an opportunity to practice new, specific, strategies. Finish by setting a time in the future to evaluate, modify, and discuss the effectiveness of each strategy.

ACTIVITY 3.10: STRESS RELIEF

Minimally stressful:

Moderately stressful:

Extremely stressful:

Currently, I do the following things to relieve stress successfully…

Specific stressor…	Specific strategy…
1.	
2.	
3.	
4.	

Date To Review Strategies: _____

ACTIVITY 3.11: RESTAURANT PREPARATION

Purpose

To practice and prepare for the demands of a family restaurant outing.

Materials needed

CD track 22, CD player, writing materials, restaurant items and props, table and chairs if needed

People needed

As many of the family members going to the restaurant as possible

Procedure

Begin by discussing past family trips to restaurants and some of the positive and negative experiences each family member has had on restaurant outings. Ask questions to determine how often the family goes out, where they go, with whom, and which restaurants they would like to visit in the future.

Have the family choose a restaurant they would like to work on preparing for. Encourage the family members to set a realistic date for this outing and try to list as many of the actual people who will go on the outing as possible. Involve the individual with autism as much as you can in the family's decision-making process and document ideas and goals on the Activity 3.11: Restaurant Preparation form.

Next, have the family members discuss their strengths as well as the perceived obstacles and concerns they may have going into the restaurant outing. Then have the family members choose five specific things they want to concentrate on in the role play (for example, "eye contact," "waiting patiently," "loud vocalizations," etc.). Document these on the Activity 3.11: Restaurant Preparation form.

Begin the role play using as many props and materials associated with restaurants as possible. Have the family assign roles (waiter or waitress, host or hostess, etc.) and be open to switching roles in the scenario from time to time. Encourage the participants to focus on the five areas they set out to work on in the role play and begin playing out the restaurant scene.

After the role-play scenario is complete, ask the family to discuss what worked well and what areas may need more practice before heading to the restaurant on the given date. Also, ask the family to set a specific date and time to practice the role play again to help ensure a successful outing. Document information on the Activity 3.11: Restaurant Preparation form.

If families enjoy this activity encourage them to try using Activity 3.2: A Trip to the… to prepare for other life events.

ACTIVITY 3.11: RESTAURANT PREPARATION

The restaurant we have chosen…

When we will go…

Who will likely go with us…

Our family's strengths…

Our restaurant obstacles and concerns…

Let's practice…

1.

2.

3.

4.

5.

What worked well…

What needs more rehearsal…

Date we will practice our restaurant trip again on: _____

ACTIVITY 3.12: SIBLING SUPPORT

Purpose

To help families consider and support the needs of siblings of individuals with autism.

Materials needed

Writing materials

People needed

Sibling(s) of the individual with ASD and as many from the family as possible

Procedure

Begin a discussion with the family, specifically with the sibling(s), about their strengths and interests. Ask him to share what autism means to them and how they think autism affects their family. Encourage participants to document thoughts and ideas on the Activity 3.12: Sibling Support form.

Next, facilitate a discussion with the sibling(s) and parents about their wishes for the family. These can include things they wish to do but cannot due to family limitations associated with ASD. However, special care should be given to encourage the siblings to think beyond autism and dream freely about their family's future (for example, "going on a cruise," "going to more movies," "moving to a new home," etc.). Have each sibling document family wishes on the Activity 3.12: Sibling Support form.

Then ask each sibling to think about general and specific ways in which their family can better support their personal needs and ways in which they can help to better support their family. Have each sibling document ways to help out on the Activity 3.12: Sibling Support form.

Finally, have the siblings choose either wishes for the family, specific supports they need, specific support they can give, or a combination of all three to role-play. The family can then practice or role-play going on different outings, offering support during difficult times, or asking for help from other family members in specific situations when support is needed.

ACTIVITY 3.12: SIBLING SUPPORT

My interests and strengths…

Autism is…

Autism impacts my family by…

I wish my family…

1.

2.

3.

4.

My family can help me by…

I can help my family by…

ACTIVITY 3.13: THE OTHER EIGHT HOURS

Purpose

To open dialog between home and school, and to begin a cooperative appreciation for the issues parents and teachers face. Use this exercise in conjunction with Activity 2.12: The Other 16 Hours.

Materials needed

Writing materials

People needed

Two or more; ideally a mix of an individual's parents and teachers

Procedure

Teamwork and team-building is essential to successful support of individuals with ASD. Collaboration between home and school is critical. Sometimes a lack of understanding of the issues faced in each environment can lead to tension and miscommunication. This role play is designed to allow each team member to develop an understanding of the issues faced across environments for an individual with ASD, and to work as a group to develop new support strategies. Special care should be given during facilitation to promote respect and avoid arguments.

Step 1

Have teachers complete the first section of the Activity 3.13: The Other Eight Hours form by writing down specific issues they face at school.

Step 2

Assign roles for the role play. A teacher should play the role of the child, as he or she knows the specific issues and how to role-play them. Have one parent play the role of the teacher. Set the scene with any props or specific information the players will need.

Step 3

Role-play as many scenarios from the Activity 3.13: The Other Eight Hours form as possible.

Step 4

Discuss the role-play scenarios. Talk as a group about discoveries, questions, or ideas that came up during the role play and document on the Activity 3.13: The Other Eight Hours form.

Step 5

If teachers want suggestions, discuss the issues as a team and work to develop potential strategies for the issues faced at school. Document on the Activity 3.13: The Other Eight Hours form.

ACTIVITY 3.13: THE OTHER EIGHT HOURS

Teachers document specific issues faced at school…

1.

2.

3.

4.

Discoveries about school during the role-play scenarios…

Potential school strategies developed by the team…

ACTIVITY 3.14: IT'S AN AUDITORY PROCESS—HOME

Purpose

To develop an awareness of auditory processing issues and modify interaction strategies for individuals with ASD.

Materials needed

CD tracks 23–25, CD player, writing materials

People needed

One or more

Procedure

Begin by discussing auditory processing issues as they relate to ASD. Use supplementary materials to describe auditory processing disorder to those who may not be familiar with the term. Ask participants to share any personal experiences they may have had with children with processing delays. Then choose a participant to play the role of the child. Play the CD for each scenario or generate your own scripts to role-play the scenarios. Document how it felt to try to respond in the role play for each scenario on the Activity 3.14: It's an Auditory Process—Home form.

1. Track 23, Echo
2. Track 24, Delay
3. Track 25, Script with no delays or issues

Then facilitate a discussion about how we, as parents, can make adjustments to the environment to support individuals with auditory processing issues, and document tips and strategies on the Activity 3.14: It's an Auditory Process—Home form.

ACTIVITY 3.14: IT'S AN AUDITORY PROCESS—HOME

My experiences with auditory processing issues…

My reactions to the role-play scenarios…

Echo:

Delay:

Script with no delays or issues:

Adjustments I can make with my child…

ACTIVITY 3.15: WORDS, WORDS, WORDS

Purpose

To simplify instructions and feedback used with individuals with ASD.

Materials needed

CD tracks 26–28, CD player, writing materials

People needed

Two or more

Procedure

Begin a discussion about the emphasis we often place on verbal feedback and how this may cause problems when working with some individuals with ASD. Ask participants to describe a time when they used too much verbal feedback with a student or child. Also ask them to describe a time when they were able to communicate meaningfully with a student or child using no words at all. Record notes on the Activity 3.15: Words, Words, Words form. Determine who will play the role of the child, and play the CD for each condition below.

Track 26, Instructions

As the person role-playing the child listens to this particular track he must do his best to execute the chain of instructions given on the CD. Following the exercise, have a discussion about the role play and document notes on the Activity 3.15: Words, Words, Words form.

Track 27, Corrections

As the person role-playing the child listens to this particular track, she must do her best to execute the chain of instructions and make the suggested correction given on the CD. Following the exercise, have a discussion about the role play and document notes on the Activity 3.15: Words, Words, Words form.

Track 28, Feedback

As the person role-playing the child listens to this particular track, he must do his best to remember three key points given in the feedback on the CD. When the track ends, the participant must retell three or more key points from the feedback to the whole group. Following the exercise, have a discussion about the role play and document notes on the Activity 3.15: Words, Words, Words form.

For training purposes, the examples on the CD are accentuated and embellished beyond what most caregivers demonstrate when working with individuals with ASD.

ACTIVITY 3.15: WORDS, WORDS, WORDS

A time I used too many words:

A time I was able to communicate using no words at all:

Track 26, Instructions

Problem:

Future solutions:

Track 27, Corrections

Problem:

Future solutions:

Track 28, Feedback

Three or more key points:

How to simplify:

ACTIVITY 3.16: TOUGH DAY PLAYBACK

Purpose

To talk through an event that was difficult, watch it played out by others, and develop new strategies regarding the situation through observation and practice.

Materials needed

Writing materials for note-taking

People needed

Three or more

Procedure

Begin by asking the participants to think about a time that was particularly difficult for her. Inform the participant that she will be asked to share the event or time with the group and only needs to share relevant information for the role play (no names or specific information that could be too difficult). When possible, shape the conversation toward a very specific difficulty that happened in the recent past. Inform the listeners to focus very closely on the details of the story as some of them will be asked to play characters from the tough day.

Once the participant sharing the story is ready to begin, prepare to make an outline of her story with critical details on large paper or some other writing area.

After she has delivered the story and notes have been collected:

1. Determine how many role-players will be needed to re-enact the story.

2. Discuss the outline you have generated and make sure with the participant that the outline reflects the event truthfully.

3. Assign roles to other participants; the storyteller will observe the playback.

4. Have the participants play back the story according to their perception of the events, using the outline to shape the role play if needed.

5. Repeat the role play if necessary to refine the events or to include moments the storyteller left out and wants to include.

After the role play has been completed:

1. Ask the original storyteller to discuss how it felt to watch others play out the scenario. Encourage her to make notes on the Activity 3.16: Tough Day Playback form.

2. Ask the original storyteller to discuss moments from the role play that surprised or encouraged her. Encourage her to make notes on the Activity 3.16: Tough Day Playback form.

Next, have the original storyteller join the role play but as a different character, not as herself.

1. Ask the original storyteller to discuss how it felt to play out the scenario as someone else. Encourage her to make notes on the Activity 3.16: Tough Day Playback form.

2. Ask the original storyteller to discuss ways she might handle similar situations in the future. Encourage her to make notes on the Activity 3.16: Tough Day Playback form.

ACTIVITY 3.16: TOUGH DAY PLAYBACK

Watching others play out my story made me think/feel...

I was surprised or encouraged when I saw...

When I played someone else in my story, it made me think/feel...

In the future I might...

ACTIVITY 3.17: GOOD DAY PLAYBACK

Purpose

To talk through an event that was positive, watch it played out by others, and assess strengths regarding the situation through observation and practice.

Materials needed

Writing materials for note-taking

People needed

Three or more

Procedure

Begin by asking the participant to think about a time that was particularly exciting or positive for him. Inform the participant that he will be asked to share the event or time with the group and only need to share relevant information for the role play (no names or specific information that could be uncomfortable). When possible, shape the conversation toward a very specific positive event that happened in the recent past. Inform the listeners to focus very closely on the details of the story as some of them will be asked to play characters from the tough day.

Once the participant sharing the story is ready to begin, prepare to make an outline of his story with critical details on large paper or some other writing area.

After he has delivered the story and notes have been collected:

1. Determine how many role-players will be needed to re-enact the story.
2. Discuss the outline you have generated and make sure with the participant that the outline reflects the event truthfully.
3. Assign roles to other participants; the storyteller will observe the playback.
4. Have the participants play back the story according to their perception of the events, using the outline to shape the role play if needed.
5. Repeat the role play if necessary to refine the events or to include moments the storyteller left out and wants to include.

After the role play has been completed:

1. Ask the original storyteller to discuss how it felt to watch others play out the scenario. Encourage him to make notes on the Activity 3.17: Good Day Playback form.
2. Ask the original storyteller to discuss moments from the role play that surprised or encouraged him. Encourage him to make notes on the Activity 3.17: Good Day Playback form.

Next, ask the original storyteller to join the role play but as a different character, not as herself.

1. Ask the original storyteller to discuss how it felt to play out the scenario as someone else. Encourage him to make notes on the Activity 3.17: Good Day Playback form.
2. Ask the original storyteller to discuss ways they might use the positive experience in the future. Encourage him to make notes on the Activity 3.17: Good Day Playback form.

ACTIVITY 3.17: GOOD DAY PLAYBACK

Watching others play out my story made me think/feel...

I was surprised or encouraged when I saw...

When I played someone else in my story it made me think/feel...

In the future I might...

ACTIVITY 3.18: PUSH-PULL

Purpose

To use physical-vocal exploration to examine the barriers impeding independence.

Materials needed

Bright tape or a rope

People needed

Two or more

Procedure

Begin by discussing the issue of independence for individuals with autism. What are the natural barriers in society and the environment? What are common social or behavioral barriers to independence? Then begin to discuss limitations we as parents have placed on the individual based on our fears or beliefs. Document these ideas on the Activity 3.18: Push-Pull form. Next, take a bright piece of tape or rope and place it in the room in an area with enough room for movement. This line will become the line between dependence and independence. Describe to the participants that they will be gently pushing and pulling their partner from that line of independence.

1. Practice gently pulling and pushing your role-playing partner in the space. Develop a comfortable and controlled physical interaction style. One person will role-play the individual with autism and others will role-play as caregivers.

2. Begin by asking the caregiver(s) to imagine a time when she limited an individual's independence and to give the moment a simple sentence: for example, "I was afraid they would fail." Ask her to develop a simple sentence that reflects the independence the person with autism was trying to achieve: for example, "I want to live on my own." Document these ideas on the Activity 3.18: Push-Pull form.

3. Have the participant playing the individual with autism start walking toward the tape or rope line, and the participant playing the caregiver gently pull her partner back from the line. Also have the pulling participant imagine, but not speak, the simple sentence she generated in step 2.

4. Repeat the above process. This time ask the participant playing the caregiver to speak her simple sentence as she pulls her role-playing partner back from the line. Also ask the participant playing the individual with autism to speak her simple sentence of independence.

5. Repeat this sequence 3–5 times in fluid and continuous loops so the caregiver participant pulls and verbalizes her fear and the participant playing the individual with autism verbalizes her sentence of independence several times in a fluid sequence.

6. Stop and discuss the role play and strategies for the future to promote and encourage independence. Document these ideas on the Activity 3.18: Push-Pull form.

ACTIVITY 3.18: PUSH-PULL

Some common societal or environmental barriers to independence are…

Some common social or behavioral barriers to independence are…

Some ways my fears or beliefs have limited an individual's independence…

Barrier sentences that might describe my fear or belief ("What If They Fail?")…

Sentences that describe what independence the individual with autism was working to achieve ("I Want To Live On My Own")…

How I can change my thoughts or actions to encourage an individual's independence in the future…

ACTIVITY 3.19: THE STRANGER

Purpose

To experience foreign social customs or behaviors and to empathize with those who may struggle to decode our social world.

Materials needed

Writing materials

People needed

Between 3 and 15

Procedure

Begin by having one participant volunteer to play the role of the stranger. Ask the participant to leave the room until the other participants have finished preparing for the rest of the role play. Inform him that you will cue him when it is time to return. Also, instruct him that when he does return all he is asked to do is interact with his peers normally. Next, work with the remaining group to develop 2–3 customs that the "stranger" would have no way of knowing. Explain that these customs should be simple, yet quite different from "everyday behavior." Help the group discover customs using the following guidelines:

1. A strange language

The group (minus the stranger) should develop a simple language to use as a group. For example, the group could speak only in verbs, use sounds only, or speak only in adjectives. Have the group practice speaking in their new, strange language and document the language specifics on the Activity 3.19: The Stranger form.

2. Strange physical behavior

The group should also develop a few strange non-verbal, physical behaviors. For example, the group could blink excessively or pull on their ears anytime they begin speaking, etc. Have the group practice speaking in their new, strange language and using strange physical behaviors. Document the behavior specifics on the Activity 3.19: The Stranger form.

3. Laughing at something the stranger does

Help the group choose something simple the stranger may do to laugh at during the role play. For example, the group could choose to laugh anytime the stranger took a step, sat down, spoke, gestured, etc. Have the group practice speaking in their strange language, using strange physical behaviors, and preparing to laugh at the stranger. Document which behavior the group will laugh at on the Activity 3.19: The Stranger form.

Prepare the group and have the participant role-playing the stranger return to the space. Let the role play unfold for 3–10 minutes. Stop the role play at a natural place. Discuss reactions on the part of the stranger to the way the role play felt and what sort of conclusions he tried to make as the scenario unfolded. Relate these conclusions to how an individual on the autism spectrum may feel in the actual social realm. Also, discuss the reactions of the group as to how it felt to exclude someone, talk around them, and ignore their confusion. Document all reactions on the Activity 3.19: The Stranger form.

ACTIVITY 3.19: THE STRANGER

Our strange language…

Our strange physical behavior(s)…

We will laugh when the stranger…

The role play made the participant playing the stranger feel…

How this might relate to an individual on the autism spectrum…

Playing a member of the large group made me feel…

ACTIVITY 3.20: MY CHILD'S DREAM

Purpose

To identify with an individual's dream and develop ideas to support that dream.

Materials needed

Writing materials

People needed

One or more

Procedure

Begin talking with the participant(s) about their child. Discuss the child's interests and strengths, things she talks about often or does particularly well. Ask the participant(s) to begin to walk in the shoes of the child. Encourage each participant to think about what sort of career their child would like to pursue, where she would prefer to live, places she dreams of visiting, or achievements she seeks. Have each participant reflect to ensure they are dreaming *as* the child and not *for* the child, and document discoveries on the Activity 3.20: My Child's Dream form.

Next, have the participants choose a handful of details from their child's dreams to role-play. Have them choose a career, an achievement, a quote, or sentences that the child may say in her life, and an action that represents one or more of those dreams. For example, their child may dream of accepting the Nobel Prize. The role-playing participant could walk from the audience to the podium, receive the award, and say a few words of thanks. Encourage participants to look at their notes to find actions, words, and emotions from their child's dream to role-play and begin.

After the participants have played one or more moments from their child's dream, have them reflect on how it felt to say, do, and feel something as their child. Document reactions on the Activity 3.20: My Child's Dream form.

Conclude by asking participants to think of ways they can discuss future dreams with their child and how they can support their child in the pursuit of those dreams. Document strategies and ideas on the Activity 3.20: My Child's Dream form.

ACTIVITY 3.20: MY CHILD'S DREAM

My child dreams of being a...

My child dreams of living...

My child dreams of seeing/doing...

...I believe these are their dreams, not my dreams for them.

Saying, doing, and feeling something as my child made me realize...

I can help foster my child's dreams by...

Chapter 4

ROLE PLAY FOR PEERS

Case Study: Jennifer's Interactions in the Gentle Coach Role Play

Jennifer was a fourth grade student in a public school. She, along with two or three peers, had been going to school with their classmate Robby for over four years. Robby was a fellow fourth grader who primarily used Picture Exchange Communication System (PECS) to communicate his wants and needs. Jennifer had truly befriended Robby and was a terrific peer model and partner for him all throughout their school years together.

Certain issues developed as the friends became older. Some of the interaction styles that were appropriate when they were younger were no longer appropriate. Excessive hugging, holding hands, talking in high-pitched baby voices, and other behaviors that were perfectly normal in kindergarten or first grade were no longer socially appropriate. Robby had also developed some boundary issues with others in his life (getting too close to others, physical touch, etc.) and his team thought it would be a good idea to help him learn appropriate boundaries as soon as possible.

Because Jennifer was one of Robby's best friends and interacted with him frequently, the team wanted to help her develop some new age-appropriate interaction strategies. Robby's paraprofessional knew Jennifer well and was able to guide her through the Gentle Coach role play to help her practice some new skills and social phrases to use with Robby. For instance, Jennifer learned to pat Robby's back instead of giving hugs when she was proud of him. She learned to use lower pitches and more natural tones with her voice when talking to Robby. She also learned how to correct Robby gently if he was getting too close or needed to use his PECS to make a request instead of grabbing her.

The role-play scenario helped Jennifer modify her interactions with Robby, which in turn helped him learn new boundaries with his peers.

ACTIVITY 4.1: TELL SOMEONE ABOUT AUTISM

Purpose

To give peers an opportunity to practice talking with others in their school or community about autism.

Materials needed

Writing materials

People needed

Two or more peers

Procedure

Begin by having a general discussion about autism with the group to get a sense of where the participants are in terms of their knowledge, questions, fears, joys, and experiences with autism. Guide the group to discuss specific interactions they have had with peers or people in their community that have an autism diagnosis, or conversations they have had with others about autism. After some discussion, pose the question "What would you tell a friend if they asked you what autism was?" and have the participants role-play telling another participant their response. Then, use the following template to construct a loose outline for those participants who know little about autism or who struggle to share a definition with others.

1. Strengths

Talk about some of the strengths that an individual might have because of their autism. Ask participants to talk about something that they have seen a friend with autism do well (painting, smiling, playing video games, playing music, etc.).

2. Challenges

Talk about the challenges some of their friends with autism have with communication, social skills, and play, and give examples for each (non-verbal, auditory processing issues, understanding emotions, fixation on one topic or activity).

3. Respect

Help the participant find as many interesting or cool things they can about their friends with autism, but also the things he or she has in common with them.

4. Tag line

Discuss things the participants might say as a way to finish the conversation about autism with a positive spin. Work on summarizing their thoughts into a simple, supportive general statement about autism or their friends with autism.

Participants can document their ideas on the Activity 4.1: Tell Someone About Autism form. The general script or outline can then be role-played until participants feel they could answer the question "what is autism?" comfortably.

ACTIVITY 4.1: TELL SOMEONE ABOUT AUTISM

Some of my friends with autism are really good at…

We all have challenges. Someone with autism might struggle with…

But I respect my friend with autism because…

We are alike in some ways too…

I think autism is…

Or

I think my friend with autism is…

ACTIVITY 4.2: INTERACTIONS

Purpose

To help peers practice interaction strategies that may increase play or communication opportunities with their peers with autism.

Materials needed

Writing materials

People needed

Two or more

Procedure

Talk with participants about general experiences they have had with classmates with autism, or if they know of any friends that have autism. If peers struggle with this step, reinforce with the Activity 4.1: Tell Someone About Autism. Then discuss how some peers with autism may need more time to respond to questions, or might need us to modify how we interact with them in order to have a successful exchange. Share with the participants that they will be working on strategies for talking with and responding to their friends with autism. Emphasize that not all of their peers with autism are the same, and that some strategies might not work or be needed with some of their friends.

1. Simplify

Have the role-play participants greet one another and ask one another social questions for several exchanges. After they have finished, discuss how some of their peers with autism respond better to simple phrases or questions. Have them think about ways that they could change the greetings and conversation from the previous role play to make it more simple and concrete. Document changes on the Activity 4.2: InterActions form and role-play the skill again.

2. Simplify without talking down

Discuss our tendency to talk to individuals with autism as though they were much younger than they really are. Remind participants that their peers may need simplified conversations or questions, but that the tones they use with their typical peers should also be used with their friends with autism. Practice the simplified role play again, being mindful of tone and document cues or reminders on the Activity 4.2: InterActions form.

3. Give them time

Talk about the importance of giving individuals with autism ample time to respond to our questions or social greetings. Also discuss how many peers do not wait long enough for a response and move on before the friend with autism can respond. Have participants think back to their original interactions and make a guess about the time elapsed between questions/comments and responses. Ask participants to practice doubling or tripling the time spent waiting/responding and document reactions on the Activity 4.2: InterActions form.

ACTIVITY 4.2: INTERACTIONS

I use some of the following phrases when I talk with friends...

I can simplify some of them by saying...

...Instead.

I can remind myself to talk normally with all of my friends by...

I can give some of my friends more time to respond by...

...and some friends might not need more time.

ACTIVITY 4.3: DEFEND A FRIEND

Purpose

To help participants develop positive strategies when standing up for peers or themselves and to give them a chance to implement those strategies.

Materials needed

Writing materials

People needed

Two or more

Procedure

Begin the activity by discussing bullying, teasing, or other negative social interactions the participants may have witnessed or experienced at school or in the community. If appropriate, discuss how those experiences made them feel and what strategies they used to handle those situations. Then, as a group, develop a list of appropriate, non-violent things they can say or do to defend a friend or themselves should they have to. Document suggestions on a large sheet of paper or writing surface placed near the performing area.

Enlist a co-facilitator to help with the next step. Inform the participants that they will be trying out some of their strategies. Model the bullying or teasing with the co-facilitator and coach the participants to approach the situation and deliver one of the appropriate suggestions listed in the group exercise or one of their own. Then have the participants repeat the process while adding a verbalization or physical move to remove themselves and their peer from the situation. Example: "I don't like the way you're talking to (Sam). Come on (Sam), let's go."

After the role play, have the participants define "bullying." Then begin a discussion about how it felt to stand up for a friend or for themselves when someone was teasing or bullying them. Talk about non-violent solutions to bullying as well. Finally, ask participants to think about who they might talk to should bullying occur.

ACTIVITY 4.3: DEFEND A FRIEND

> I define bullying as…

> How does it feel to stand up to bullying?

> What non-violent strategies can I use?

> Who can I talk to about someone bullying me or my friends?

ACTIVITY 4.4: THE GENTLE COACH

Purpose

To support peers of individuals with autism by teaching them strategies for interacting naturally throughout the school day.

Materials needed

Writing materials

People needed

Two or more

Procedure

Begin a discussion with typical peers, and peers with autism if appropriate, about the importance of being able to offer our friends with autism the same kind of support we offer other friends. Talk about how the needs and approaches may be different but the overall interaction style is the same. Describe how sometimes peers overreact or underreact to their peers with autism. Stress the importance of being natural.

Then discuss the specific strengths and interests of their peers with autism and some of the ways they have helped them in the past. Next, talk about events, occurrences, and social situations that might be difficult for their friends with autism. Document all ideas on the Activity 4.4: The Gentle Coach form.

Role Play

1. Have one participant play himself and another participant play the role of the peer with autism. Practice explaining a difficult concept from the Activity 4.4: The Gentle Coach form to the participant playing the peer with autism. Guide the practicing participant to use concrete terms with his peer with autism but to avoid talking loudly, condescendingly, or unnaturally to his peer.

2. Again, have one participant play himself and another participant play the role of the peer with autism. Have the practicing participant demonstrate a difficult social skill from the Activity 4.4: The Gentle Coach form for the peer with autism using the same natural, but concrete, interaction styles.

3. Role-play a conversation between the practicing participant and the participant playing the peer with autism. Coach the practicing participant to talk to the peer naturally. If the peer with autism is non-verbal, have the practicing participant use simple but natural, age-appropriate language to interact.

4. Role-play introducing the peer with autism to another peer or a group of peers. Have the practicing participant use language and styles he would use to introduce someone naturally.

Document reactions and ideas on the Activity 4.4: The Gentle Coach form.

ACTIVITY 4.4: THE GENTLE COACH

My friend with autism is really good at…

They like to…

Right now I help my friend by…

They may not understand when these things happen (concepts)…

They may not understand when someone does this (social skill)…

How I can explain difficult things…

How I can demonstrate difficult things…

How I can treat my friend just like my other friends…

How I can connect my friend with autism to new friends…

ACTIVITY 4.5: BUS BULLY

Purpose

To practice recognizing and dealing appropriately with bullies on the bus.

Materials needed

CD track 29, CD player, chairs, school materials, writing materials

People needed

Three or more

Procedure

Begin by asking participants general questions about the bullying they see in their schools and communities. Role-playing Activity 4.3: Defend a Friend before this role play may help set necessary foundation skills. Discuss reasons individuals with autism may be bullied, and have the participants reflect on their own experiences regarding their friends with autism. Next, ask the participants to consider why bullying might occur on the school bus, and ask peers to share specific things bullies might do on the bus. Record ideas and thoughts on the Activity 4.5: Bus Bully form.

Then assign roles so that at least one participant is playing the bully, the peer, and the friend with autism. Begin the role play using chairs, the CD, and other props if needed, and ask the participant playing the bully to engage in bullying behaviors toward the individual role-playing the friend with autism. Stop the role play after some time and ask the participants to update the Activity 4.5: Bus Bully form with any new bullying behaviors they saw.

As a group, discuss safe steps participants can take if they see someone bullying a friend with autism. Also, have the participants generate specific safe things to say to bullies should an incident occur. Write the specific safe steps and phrases on the Activity 4.5: Bus Bully form.

Switch roles and restart the role play. This time have participants role-play using both their safe steps and safe phrases during the role play to practice and prepare for real bullying events.

End the role-play activity by asking participants to list the positive things they can share with others about their friend with autism to help reduce bullying and increase acceptance on the bus and in their school or community.

ACTIVITY 4.5: BUS BULLY

My friends with autism might be bullied because…

Ways that kids might bully others on the bus…

Safe steps I can take if I see someone bullying my friends with autism…

1.

2.

3.

4.

Safe things I can say to a bully on the bus…

Positive things I can share with others about my friend with autism…

ACTIVITY 4.6: SENSORY OVERLOAD

Purpose

To bring awareness and sensitivity to some of the auditory sensory issues peers with autism may face.

Materials needed

CD tracks 33–35 and track 43 for British introduction, CD player, writing materials

People needed

One or more

Procedure

Discuss how some peers with autism may have significant sensory issues. Talk about how sensory processing problems can dramatically impact many areas of an individual's life such as learning, communication, play, and community participation. Ask the participants to share smells, sounds, tastes, or sights that are unpleasant to them. Then help the participants connect their own reactions to the hypersensitivity individuals with autism may experience. Inform the role-players that they will be listening to some sounds to get a better feel for some of the challenges peers with autism may face.

1. Introduction

Use the CD Sensory Overload Introduction track (30 or 43) to introduce participants to some of the sound sensitivity issues their friends with ASD may face. Have participants document smells, sounds, tastes, or sights that they dislike on the Activity 4.6: Sensory Overload form.

2. School work

Use the CD Sensory Overload School Work track (31) to have role-players attempt to complete an academic task (chosen by the facilitator beforehand) while distracting sounds play. Have participants document on the Activity 4.6: Sensory Overload form personal reactions to the exercise, how sensory issues may affect learning, and what they could do to help reduce sensory challenges in the classroom for their friends with autism.

3. Socialization

Use the CD Sensory Overload Socialization track (32) to have role-players attempt to talk or play with a friend while distracting sounds play. Have participants document on the Activity 4.6: Sensory Overload form personal reactions to the exercise, how sensory issues may affect socialization, and what they could do to help reduce sensory challenges during play or social times for their friends with autism.

ACTIVITY 4.6: SENSORY OVERLOAD

The smells, tastes, sounds, and sights that bother me are…

School work:

My personal reactions to the exercise…

How sensory issues might affect learning…

What I can do to help reduce sensory challenges in the classroom for my friends with autism…

Socialization:

My personal reactions to the exercise…

How sensory issues might affect socialization…

What I can do to help reduce sensory challenges in social situations for my friends with autism…

ACTIVITY 4.7: IT'S AN AUDITORY PROCESS—PLAYGROUND

Purpose

To develop an awareness of auditory processing issues and to modify interaction strategies for individuals with ASD.

Materials needed

CD tracks 33–35 (US), 44–46 (British), CD player, writing materials

People needed

One or more

Procedure

Begin by discussing auditory processing issues as they relate to ASD. Use supplementary materials to describe auditory processing disorder to those who may not be familiar with the term. Ask participants to share any personal experiences they may have had with peers who took time to respond or did not seem to respond, for example, to play requests. Then choose a participant to play the role of the peer with autism. Play the CD for each scenario, or generate your own scripts to role-play the scenarios. Document how it felt to try to respond in the role play for each scenario on the Activity 4.7: It's an Auditory Process—Playground form.

1. Track 33/44, Echo
2. Track 34/35, Delay
3. Track 35/36, Script with no delays or issues

Then facilitate a discussion about how peers make adjustments to their interaction strategies to support individuals with auditory processing issues, and document tips and strategies on the Activity 4.7: It's an Auditory Process—Playground form.

ACTIVITY 4.7: IT'S AN AUDITORY PROCESS—PLAYGROUND

My experiences with my friends or classmates with autism…

My reactions to the role-play scenarios…

Echo:

Delay:

Script with no delays or issues:

Adjustments I can make with my friends…

ACTIVITY 4.8: JUST AS I AM

Purpose

To empathize with others, embrace others' differences, and embrace what is different within one's self.

Materials needed

Writing materials

People needed

Two or more; ideally some with and some without an ASD diagnosis

Procedure

Begin by having the participants discuss and write down things that make them different from others. Encourage them to explore aspects of themselves such as wearing glasses, having freckles, being tall or short, having asthma or allergies, liking funny foods, having an illness, or having a disability. Encourage the participants to write down their ideas on the Activity 4.8: Just as I Am form. Inform them that you will be collecting the forms and handing them out to others to read.

Assure participants that this will be a safe exercise by establishing the following ground rules:

1. We will uplift and respect one another by listening and participating.
2. We will celebrate one another's differences and encourage others.
3. We will keep our environment safe and free of teasing or bullying.
4. We will treat the information others share with respect and dignity, and will not share information with others without the consent of each role-player.
5. We will accept one another Just As We Are.

Assign each Activity 4.8: Just as I Am form to someone other than the original author. Give a moment for each to look at their new form. Then, one by one, have participants read their new form. End each presentation with applause and celebration.

Finish by discussing reactions to:

1. hearing someone read their form.
2. reading someone else's form.

Document reactions on the participant's Activity 4.8: Just as I Am form.

ACTIVITY 4.8: JUST AS I AM

Script

My name is…

You and I have a lot in common. But we are different as well. I have…

So, there are probably some things about me that make me different from you. But we have to remember that we all have at least one thing in common—we all need help from one another to get through life. Please accept me Just as I Am!

Things I learned when reading…

Things I learned when listening to mine being read…

ACTIVITY 4.9: THAT'S NOT FAIR!

Purpose

To work through issues peers may have with accommodations, supports, and special interactions their friends with autism may receive.

Materials needed

Writing materials

People needed

Two or more

Procedure

Begin a discussion with typical peers, and peers with autism, if appropriate, about the issues that typical peers have raised about the fairness of some of the supports their peers with autism receive (candy, reduced work, help from aides, etc.). Also discuss with peers why they believe parents or teachers use those techniques to support their peers with autism. Have the participants document these concerns on the Activity 4.9: That's Not Fair! form.

Revisit the perceived strengths and struggles of peers with autism with the participants, and have them document those on the Activity 4.9: That's Not Fair! form.

Next, begin a role-play scenario where one participant plays the role of a peer with autism and an adult or peer plays the role of caregiver (teacher, aide, or parent).

1. Start a simple activity that highlights one of the perceived struggles of their peer (handwriting, self-care, testing, etc.).

2. Have the participant role-playing the caregiver withhold support for a short time.

3. Next have the participant playing the caregiver use one of the discussed support strategies for a short time.

4. Switch roles so that each participant plays the caregiver and peer with autism.

Finally, end by asking participants to discuss something they struggle with and what supports they receive from others to accomplish tasks associated with that struggle. Have the participants document these supports and reactions on the Activity 4.9: That's Not Fair! form. Facilitate a conversation about the connections and reactions participants have made during the role-play scenario.

ACTIVITY 4.9: THAT'S NOT FAIR!

Sometimes I become upset when teachers or parents…

I feel they do those things for my peer with autism because…

My peer with autism is very good at…

My peer with autism struggles with…

When I played the role of my peer with autism, teachers or parents helped me by…

This felt…

I sometimes struggle with…

Others help me by…

ACTIVITY 4.10: THE STRANGER

Purpose

To experience foreign social customs or behaviors and to empathize with those who may struggle to decode our social world.

Materials needed

Writing materials

People needed

Between 3 and 15

Procedure

Begin by having one participant volunteer to play the role of the stranger. Ask the participant to leave the room until the other participants have finished preparing for the rest of the role play. Inform her that you will cue her when it is time to return. Also, instruct her that when she does return all she is asked to do is interact with her peers normally. Next, work with the remaining group to develop 2–3 customs that the "stranger" would have no way of knowing. Explain that these customs should be simple, yet quite different from "everyday behavior." Help the group discover customs using the following guidelines:

1. A strange language

The group (minus the stranger) should develop a simple language to use as a group. For example, the group could speak only in verbs, use sounds only, or speak only in adjectives. Have the group practice speaking in their new, strange language and document the language specifics on the Activity 4.10: The Stranger form.

2. Strange physical behavior

The group should also develop a few strange non-verbal, physical behaviors. For example, the group could blink excessively or pull on their ears anytime they begin speaking. Have the group practice speaking in their new, strange language and using strange physical behaviors. Document the behavior specifics on the Activity 4.10: The Stranger form.

3. Laughing at something the stranger does

Help the group choose something simple the stranger may do to laugh at during the role play. For example, the group could choose to laugh whenever the stranger takes a step, sits down, speaks, or gestures. Have the group practice speaking in their strange language, using strange physical behaviors, and preparing to laugh at the stranger. Document which behavior the group will laugh at on the Activity 4.10: The Stranger form.

Prepare the group and have the participant role-playing the stranger return to the space. Let the role play unfold for 3–10 minutes. Stop the role play at a natural place. Discuss reactions on the part of the stranger to the way the role play felt and what sort of conclusions she tried to make as the scenario unfolded. Relate these conclusions to how an individual on the autism spectrum may feel in the actual social realm. Also, discuss the reactions of the group as to how it felt to exclude someone, talk around them, and ignore their confusion. Document all reactions on the Activity 4.10: The Stranger form.

ACTIVITY 4.10: THE STRANGER

Our strange language…

Our strange physical behavior(s)…

We will laugh when the stranger…

The role play made the participant playing the stranger feel…

How this might relate to an individual on the autism spectrum…

Playing a member of the large group made me feel…

ACTIVITY 4.11: I DON'T UNDERSTAND

Purpose

To give peers a forum to ask questions about autism and to role-play to gain understanding.

Materials needed

Writing materials

People needed

Two or more; as many as possible

Procedure

Introduce the activity and ask participants to think about things that they find confusing, scary, different, or mysterious about autism. Also ask participants to think about questions they might have about, for example, diagnosis, therapies, or behaviors, and have them write questions or comments on the Activity 4.11: I Don't Understand form.

Once participants have thought about and written down their questions or comments, go around the group and ask each person to share a few things they have written. During this phase of the role-play encourage some of the participants to role-play or act out behaviors or confusing characteristics for others to see. Ask them how it feels to move, think, or speak like their friends with autism. Also ask participants to write down things they learned while watching others or listening to others' questions or concerns. Document reactions on the Activity 4.11: I Don't Understand form.

Then have participants write a list of things they do that are likely to be confusing to their friends with autism on the Activity 4.11: I Don't Understand form.

Discuss the importance of being able to ask questions or raise concerns should a confusing or challenging issue arise regarding autism experiences.

Plan as a group ways that participants can work together to answer difficult questions and resolve challenging issues. Also discuss ways that the group can work to include their friends with autism as much as possible in the process of questioning and resolving conflicts, and document all plans and ideas on the Activity 4.11: I Don't Understand form.

ACTIVITY 4.11: I DON'T UNDERSTAND

Questions I would like to ask about autism…

Things that are confusing, scary, different, or mysterious about autism…

How it felt to act out my questions or concerns…

What I learned from watching or listening to others' questions or concerns…

Things I do that could be confusing to my friend with autism…

Our group's plan for what to do if we have more questions and for including our friends with autism in the process…

Chapter 5

PRINTABLE TOOLS FOR FACILITATION

CUSTOM ACTIVITY

Create Your Own

Purpose:

Materials needed:

People needed:

Procedure:

CUSTOM ACTIVITY

Create Your Own

Notes...

✓

FACILITATOR PLANNING SHEET

Facilitator name:

Date:

Target group:

Individual with ASD ☐ Teacher ☐ Parent ☐ Peer ☐

What are the strengths of the role-players?

What issues do I want to address?

What activities will I use?

Do I need to custom-design an activity? (see Brainstorm form)

Who, when, and where?

Other notes:

FACILITATOR NOTES

Facilitator name:

Date:

Target group:

Individual with ASD ☐   Teacher ☐   Parent ☐   Peer ☐

What issues or skills did we address?
What activities did we use?

What worked in the role-play scenario(s)?
What needs more work or adjustment?

What's the next step?

✓

NEW ACTIVITY BRAINSTORM FORM

Facilitator name:

Date:

Target group:

Individual with ASD ☐   Teacher ☐   Parent ☐   Peer ☐

What would I like the role-player to learn from the activity?

How will I break the skill/perspective into small, teachable steps?

What should the participants document for future use?

How many people are needed?

What materials are needed?

TRACKING INDIVIDUAL PARTICIPANTS' SKILLS (TIPS)

Participant:

Date:

TIPS review date:

Skill/perspective area:

Present level:

Role-play strategies:

Plan for generalization

Skill/perspective area:

Present level:

Role-play strategies:

Plan for generalization

✓

PARTICIPANT IDEA SHEET

Name:

Date:

I would like to know more about…

I get frustrated when…

I think I am really good at…

It would help me to practice…

It would be fun to try a role play about…

REFERENCES

Ahsen, N. (2008) "Role plays to build counseling competencies." *Medical Education,* 42 (5), 534–535.

Baer, A., Freer, J., Milling, D., Potter, *et al.* (2008) "Breaking bad news: Use of cancer survivors in role-playing exercises." *Journal of Palliative Medicine,* 11 (6), 885–892.

Balen, R. and Masson, H. (2008) "The Victoria Climbié case: Social work education for practice in children and families' work before and since." *Child and Family Social Work,* 13 (2), 121–132.

Ballon, B.C., Silver, I., and Fidler, D. (2007) "Headspace theater: An innovative method for experiential learning of psychiatric symptomatology using modified role playing and improvisational theater techniques." *Academic Psychiatry,* 31 (5), 380–387.

Bielanska, A., Chechnicki, A., and Budzyna-Dawidowski, P. (1991) "Drama therapy as a means of rehabilitation for schizophrenic patients: our impressions." *American Journal of Psychotherapy,* 45 (4), 566–575.

Berard, K. and Smith, R. (2008) "Evaluating a positive parenting curriculum package: An analysis of the acquisition of key skills." *Research on Social Work Practice,* 18 (5), 442–452.

Borgia, L., Owles, C., and Marcell, B. (2008) "Terrific teaching tips." *Illinois Reading Council Journal,* 36 (3), 34–39.

Carlson, S., Tahiroglu, D., and Taylor, M. (2008) "Links between dissociation and role play in a nonclinical sample of preschool children." *Journal of Trauma and Dissociation,* 9 (2), 149–171.

Chan, J. and O'Reilly, M. (2008) "A Social Stories™ intervention package for students with autism in inclusive classroom settings." *Journal of Applied Behavior Analysis,* 41 (3), 405–409.

Day, L. (1998) "Helping children talk." *Child Health Dialogue,* 12, 11.

Eckstrom, E., Desai, S., Hunter, A., Allen, E., *et al.* (2008) "Aiming to improve care of older adults: An innovative faculty development workshop." *JGIM: Journal of General Internal Medicine,* 23 (7), 1053–1056.

Halleck, G. (2008) "Bullying: A ready-to-use simulation." *Simulation and Gaming,* 39 (2), 266–281.

Harding, C.G., Safer, L.A., Kavanagh, J., Bania, R., *et al.* (1996) "Using live theatre combined with role playing and discussion to examine what at-risk adolescents think about substance abuse, its consequences, and prevention." *Adolescence,* 31 (124), 783–796.

Hardoff, D. and Schonmann, S. (2001) "Training physicians in communication skills with adolescents using teenage actors as simulated patients." *Medical Education,* 35 (3), 188–190.

Irwin, E.C. (1977) "Play, fantasy, and symbols: Drama with emotionally disturbed children." *American Journal of Psychotherapy,* 31 (3), 426–436.

Jackson, A.M. (2003) "Follow the Fish: Involving young people in primary care in Midlothian." *Health Expect,* 6 (4), 342–351.

Jacobsen, T., Baerheim, A., Lepp, M.R., and Schei, E. (2006) "Analysis of role play in medical communication training using a theatrical device the fourth wall." *BMC Medical Education,* 6, 51.

Jones, P. (2008) "The active self: Drama therapy and philosophy." *Arts in Psychotherapy,* 35 (3), 224–231.

Joronen, K., Rankin, S.H., and Astedt-Kurki, P. (2008) "School-based drama interventions in health promotion for children and adolescents: Systematic review." *Journal of Advanced Nursing,* 63 (2), 116–131.

Kraus, R. (2008) "You must participate: Violating research ethical principles through role-play." *College Teaching,* 56 (3), 131–136.

Meltzer, B.A. (2002) "Everything I needed to know about medical management I learned in acting school." *Physician Executive,* 28 (4), 48–50.

Nicholson, H. (2005) *Applied Drama: The Gift of Theatre.* Basingstoke: Palgrave.

Pecaski and McLennan, D. (2008) "The benefits of using sociodrama in the elementary classroom: Promoting caring relationships among educators and students." *Early Childhood Education Journal,* 35 (5), 451–456.

Ramamoorthi, P. (2008) "ARTRAN conversation with co-founder Dr. Parasuram Ramamoorthi." *Official Podcast of the Applied Theatre Research and Autism Network.* Available at www.autismtheatre.org, accessed on 14 January 2010

Roscoe, E. and Fisher, W. (2008) "Evaluation of an efficient method for training staff to implement stimulus preference assessments." *Journal of Applied Behavior Analysis,* 41 (2), 249–254.

Rowan, K. (2008) "Monthly communication skill coaching for healthcare staff." *Patient Education and Counseling,* 71 (3), 402–404.

Schick, L. (2008) "Breaking frame in a role-play simulation: A language socialization perspective." *Simulation and Gaming,* 39 (2), 184–197.

Sitzer, D.I., Twamley, E.M., Patterson, T.L., and Jeste, D.V. (2008) "Multivariate predictors of social skills performance in middle-aged and older out-patients with schizophrenia spectrum disorders." *Psychological Medicine* 38, 755–763.

Stokes, T.F. and Baer, D.M. (1977) "An implicit technology of generalization." *Journal of Applied Behavior Analysis,* 10, 349–367.

"Table Tactics." (2008) *Scholastic Parent and Child,* 15 (7), 15.

Wolfberg, O.J. (2009) *Play and Imagination in Children with Autism.* Second Edition. New York, NY: Teachers College Press and Overland Park, KS: Autism Asperger Publishing Company.

CD TRACK LIST

Chapter 1

1) Supermarket Success 10:38
2) Stranger Safety—Youth 1:15
3) Stranger Safety—Teen 1:18
4) Can I Take A Message #1 0:47
5) Can I Take A Message #2 1:02
6) Can I Take A Message #3 0:57
7) Cafeteria Customs 7:04

Chapter 2

8) In the Room—Doctor 1:04
9) In the Room—Fellow Teacher 0:47
10) In the Room—Parents 1:09
11) Small Victories 1:01
12) Words, Words, Words—Instructions 0:31
13) Words, Words, Words—Corrections 0:50
14) Words, Words, Words—Feedback 0:37
15) It's An Auditory Process—Echo 1:39
16) It's An Auditory Process—Delay 1:40
17) It's An Auditory Process—
No Effect 1:40

Chapter 3

18) In the Room—Doctor 1:04
19) In the Room—Teachers 0:47
20) In the Room—Fellow Parents 1:09
21) Small Victories 1:01
22) Restaurant Preparation 5:02
23) It's An Auditory Process—Echo 0:32
24) It's An Auditory Process—Delay 0:37
25) It's An Auditory Process—No
Effect 0:32
26) Words, Words, Words—Instruction 0:37
27) Words, Words, Words—Correction 0:31
28) Words, Words, Words—Feedback 0:30

Chapter 4

29) Bus Bully 5:06
30) Sensory Overload—Introduction 1:48
31) Sensory Overload—School Work 1:00
32) Sensory Overload—Socialization 1:08
33) It's An Auditory Process—Echo 0:33
34) It's An Auditory Process—Delay 0:33
35) It's An Auditory Process—No
Effect 0:33

BONUS SOUNDS

36) Playground 6:33
37) Country Breeze 4:53

Chapter 1
ASD—British Accents

38) Stranger Safety—Youth 0:39
39) Stranger Safety—Teen 0:55
40) Can I Take A Message #1 0:29
41) Can I Take A Message #2 0:26
42) Can I Take A Message #3 0:25

Chapter 4
Peers—British Accents

43) Sensory Overload—Introduction 1:46
44) It's An Auditory Process—Echo 0:21
45) It's An Auditory Process—Delay 0:24
46) It's An Auditory Process—No
Effect 0:21